AF657224

MODI 2.0

A Resolve to Secure India

Editors

Ranjit Pachnanda
Bibek Debroy
Anirban Ganguly
Uttam Kumar Sinha

PENTAGON PRESS LLP

MODI 2.0: A Resolve to Secure India

Editors: Bibek Debroy, Ranjit Pachnanda,
Anirban Ganguly and Uttam Kumar Sinha

ISBN 978-93-90095-41-4

First Published in 2021

Copyright © RESERVED

All rights reserved. No part of this publication may be reproduced, stored in a retrieval system, or transmitted in any form or by any means, electronic, mechanical, photocopying, recording or otherwise, without the prior written permission of the Publisher.

Disclaimer: The views and opinions expressed in the book are the individual assertion of the Authors and not necessarily of SPMRF. The Publisher does not take any responsibility for the same in any manner whatsoever. The same shall solely be the responsibility of the Authors.

Published by
PENTAGON PRESS LLP
206, Peacock Lane, Shahpur Jat
New Delhi-110049
Phones: 011-64706243, 26491568
Telefax: 011-26490600
email: rajan@pentagonpress.in
website: www.pentagonpress.in

Printed at Aegean Offset Printers, Greater Nodia, U.P.

Contents

Introduction

The National Democratic Alliance (NDA) government led by Prime Minister Narendra Modi completed two years of its second term in May 2021. Seven years ago, the narrative of Indian politics shifted to laying emphasis on reform, transform and perform. Delivery of benefits and schemes to a wider reach became the bedrock of politics. With the passing years, people continue to put their trust in the NDA government. At a critical time during the COVID-19 pandemic last year when peoples' trust of popular elected leaders around the world was falling, the trust barometer level, according to a number of surveys on the Modi government was rising and higher than the governments in the USA, Japan and Canada. Now in the midst of a second wave, the government is overcoming the situation with the same spirit of responsibility.

Safety and security lie at the heart of the prosperity of a nation. Real security is not only based on growth, reform and change or, what can be described as all-round development of the nation, but also enhanced focus on the borders given the escalation of tension. On national security issues, the people's confidence in the NDA-government has been consistently high. To recall, at a public rally in Bihar in April 2019, against the backdrop of the Balakot air strikes deep in Pakistan, Narendra Modi had distinguished between two types of politics. One, he described as *'vote bhakti,'* and the other as *'desh bhakti'*. The choice for the people of India between the vote bank politics of the Congress Party with its confused secularism and policy of appeasement, on the one hand, and the uncompromising national security goals of the NDA government, on the other, was clear. The rest, as they say, is history.

The NDA-government was re-elected with a thumping majority surpassing its 2014 tally of 316 with a supreme 350 seats in the Lok Sabha. The Bharatiya Janata Party (BJP) itself won 303 seats across the country. It and its allies not only increased their respective vote shares and seat shares but also expanded their geographic reach. In fact, the BJP secured 50 per cent or more vote share in 16 states. The 'Congress System' had seen its exit.

National security is non-negotiable and there can be no room for complacency. Prime Minister Modi is not in the category of those leaders who will spend sleepless nights "agonising over the plight of terror suspects". The Prime Minister, when presented with the grave situation of cross-border terror, took a call for 'hot pursuit', thereby exhibiting his firm conviction not to 'bow down' to Pakistan-sponsored terrorists.

While trust and collaboration are central to a systematic approach to security, it is cohesively strung on three core objectives: effective diplomacy and military capabilities; bolstering economic prosperity; and providing governance and promoting democratic values. They present formidable challenges and are not easy to achieve, but under Modi's 'thinking thoroughly' leadership, there has been an earnest movement with long-term strategic planning and review.

The Strategic Policy Group (SPG) was constituted in September 2018 to assist the National Security Council (NSC) with the National Security Adviser (NSA) as its chairperson to strategize internal and economic security. The notification for it stated, "The SPG shall be the principal mechanism for inter-ministerial coordination and integration of relevant inputs in the formulation of national security policies". Other members of the SPG include the Vice-Chairman of the NITI Aayog, the Cabinet Secretary, the three Service chiefs, RBI governors, Secretaries of External Affairs, Home, Defence, Finance, Defence Production, Revenue, Atomic Energy, Space and the National Security Council Secretariat besides the Scientific Advisor to the Defence

Minister, Secretary (R) in the Cabinet Secretariat and the Intelligence Bureau Chief.

Alert to the changing threat landscape, the government reasoned that any compartmentalised or silo-driven approach to national security is out dated and required a fresh integrated approach. New institutional mechanisms and structures were put in place like the Defence Planning Commission (DPC) in April 2018 under the chairmanship of the NSA to "facilitate a comprehensive and integrated planning for defence matters." It is mandated to prepare a set of tasks and actions in consonance with priorities and resources including national security strategy, strategic defence review and doctrines, international defence engagement strategy and roadmap to build a defence manufacturing eco-system. The HQ Integrated Defence Staff (IDS), set up in 2001, now functions with clear objectives as the secretariat of the DPC. Thereon, the Prime Minister gave the green signal for the formation of the three tri-services agencies—the defence cyber agency, the defence space agency and the special operations division.

A few months before the general elections in May 2019, Prime Minister Modi took a critical decision to carry out the Anti-Satellite Test (ASAT) called 'Mission Shakti'. It signalled a move to acquire space weapons confirming in the process India's capability. Such actions instil confidence among decision-makers giving them clarity to deal with China's increasing space military inventory. The success of ASAT makes India the fourth country capable of destroying an enemy satellite after the USA, Russia and China. Thereon, in December 2019, the Cabinet approved the charter and post of chief of defence staff (CDS), a four-star general, as the principal military advisor to the Defence Minister and head of the new department of military affairs (DMA). The position of the CDS position is to ensure synergy in training, logistics and procurement of the three Services and is answerable to Parliament.

The CDS was a long-pending defence reform for over two decades but the Modi government went beyond symbolism and also created the DMA for functional effectiveness. It deals with issues exclusively related to military matters, while the Defence Ministry takes a broad view of the defence of the country. The CDS, in promoting jointness in crucial functions, has led to the creation of Integrated Theatre Commands with air defence and maritime commands. This is critical not only against the backdrop of border tensions with China on the Line of Actual Control (LAC) in eastern Ladakh and Pakistani hostility on the Line of Control (LOC) in Jammu and Kashmir but also India's muscular stance in the Indo-Pacific region where many of the "future challenges are likely to occur in, and emanate from."

India's deep-rooted democratic values and structures have ensured peaceful political transitions. It is being increasingly realised that political stability and national security are interlinked. In the seven years of the NDA-government, such stability has ensured a sustainable policy framework. A secure and confident India has been the principal driver of the NDA-government. In its second term, national security has seen a transformative and pragmatic change that reflects the aspirations of Indians to see their country as a truly great power. Pakistan has been effectively kept under restraint with sustained military and diplomatic pressures. With China, India has shown its intent without shying away from taking hard decisions. Equally important has been the emphasis on internal security with reforms in the police force corresponding to the changing challenges. Often forgotten is the fact that more than 34,000 police personnel have sacrificed their lives for maintaining internal security. What has clearly been evidenced is a growing consciousness in the government for the need of a robust national security system, both internal and external, that is well structured, efficiently managed and free of *ad hocism*.

Never before has decision-making and policy responses undergone such fundamental changes that draw in the value of pre-emptive, proactive and graded responses. Importantly, the government as a trustee in its dealing with various crises has never been so crucially significant both in terms of governance and institutional responses.

In the light of the above, the editors, under the auspices of the Dr. Syama Prasad Mookerjee Research Foundation, felt the need for a compendium that would carefully scrutinise government policies, initiations, responses to crisis, and the political leadership role.

Resultantly, this edited volume brings out a comprehensive treatment of the important aspects of national security by providing an integrated collection of chapters by authors with their experiences, achievements and wealth of knowledge.

The volume begins by contextualising Prime Minister Modi's quest for a secure India and with a sense of history, Anirban Ganguly describes the foresightedness of Dr. Syama Prasad Mookerjee, who having resigned from Jawaharlal Nehru's cabinet in April 1950 often raised the question of India's preparedness in wake of imminent external dangers. The chapters, thereon, while emphasising the security and strategic policies in many ways, also underline the Modi government's '*Sabka Saath, Sabka Vikas*' approach which, as Sarbananda Sonowal notes, "has played a magical role in building new confidence among the people." Referring to the insurgency in the Northeastern states, Sonowal writes that the government's priority has been to safeguard and uphold the interests and aspirations of the people who have been for long the "victims of perennial neglect and living in difficult conditions". The porous Indo-Bangladesh border, as he writes, had always been a concern as a result of cross-border terrorism and mentions the recent efforts of the central government to introduce 'smart technology' to monitor and seal the border and prevent illegal migration from Bangladesh. Countering cross-border terrorism has been a significant policy intervention of the Modi government.

Bibek Debroy reminds us of our ancient *raja dharma* wisdom that defines the primary responsibility of the government to protect its people from "external aggression and ensure internal security and speedy dispute resolution." He argues that the country's socio-economic and political conditions are changing the dynamics of Centre-State relations and therefore need to respond to change. Focusing on police reforms, he argues that since the nature of 'crime' has changed, a shift for the police to the Concurrent List will be in order, "so that the entire country has a unified approach towards police and the handling of crime."

Organised crime and technology advancement in safeguarding national security set the tone for the next two chapters. Satya Pal Singh perceptively notes that "Prime Minister Modi was aware about the extent and depredations of the underworld and how its nexus with politicians and bureaucrats was eroding the developmental climate of India. The Centre and the BJP-led State governments have taken various stringent measures to tackle the menace of the underworld, especially in cities, by enacting tough laws and simultaneously strengthening the police and intelligence agencies." Alok Joshi writes that one of the radical changes brought about by the Modi Government was to take a holistic view of the functioning of the security architecture. He observes, "The challenge was not only to upgrade technologies but also to ensure that they adapted to the need of the hour and delivered the results that could be operationalised. Technology was further leveraged not only to reconnect the various parts of the security establishment but also to create a feedback mechanism to ensure that the lessons learnt were incorporated to improve upon the processes put in place."

In assessing the leadership role of Prime Minister Modi in dealing with security challenges, Ranjit Pachnanda focuses on the Prime Minister's "inspirational role and sterling leadership" while examining policies towards Jammu and Kashmir (Article 370) and China. He mentions that the formation of the Union Territories of J&K and Ladakh has been a "momentous achievement to rejuvenate and resurge Indian unity and development in J&K." He observes succinctly that infrastructure development under Modi is a "national priority" and further writes, "has become a great deterrent for China" along the Indo-China border. Apart from J&K and China, the author also examines the effective way the Modi Government has dealt with Left Wing Extremism and brought peace in the Northeast.

The following chapter by Sujan Chinoy has a fascinating account of how the NDA Government endeavoured to get back stolen antiquities and notes in particular, "the personal interest taken by Prime Minister Narendra Modi in the return of stolen and illegally exported Indian art and antiquities". To illustrate his point the author cites the ASI as saying that "there had been a definite spurt in retrieving India's lost antiquities during the Modi years, whereas between 2004-2009 no such objects were brought back, and between 1976 and 2013, only a total of 13 antiquities had been brought back to India".

Considerable debate has originated about India's strategic outlook and global engagement under the stewardship of Modi. The following five chapters capture the central importance and the direction of India's strategic and security policies. R.K. Dhowan, while traversing India's maritime heritage, projects the country's vast maritime interests. He explains the concept of 'Blue Economy' arguing that the government's recent initiatives "will act as catalysts to strengthen the growth of India as a credible maritime power." He further notes that "India's vast maritime interests are also enablers of our Blue Economy, and the entire span of maritime sectors is likely to witness significant growth in the coming years, and will also serve as avenues for maritime cooperation with other neighbouring countries".

Asoke Mukerji, with his experience of serving as India's Permanent Representative to the UN, writes on how India can leverage the UN for a convention on global terrorism. The need to extradite alleged terrorists, the author argues, is a priority for India and he writes: "The Comprehensive Convention on International Terrorism (CCIT) should be seen in this context." Once adopted, the CCIT will become an international framework to counter all forms of terrorism, including trans-border activities of terrorists and terrorist entities. The need to extradite alleged terrorists if a member-state cannot or will not prosecute them is, of course, the key to the CCIT's relevance.

Sujan Chinoy, in his second chapter, peruses the global security landscape. While mentioning the COVID-19 pandemic, he observes that this "provides an opportune moment to turn the spotlight to the inherent weaknesses of the Biological Weapons Convention (BWC) of 1975." He further notes that "In the run-up to the 9th Review Conference of the BWC in 2021, India could engage in consultations with other middle powers to evolve a regime that can provide better oversight."

The security and stability of Afghanistan has always been of paramount interest to India and Amar Sinha, in his chapter, digs deep into his knowledge and experience in Afghanistan as he analyses current factors that are defining the relationship. He writes emphatically that "While Indian policies towards Afghanistan have been consistent, the arrival of Prime Minister Narendra Modi gave this relationship a new impetus. A new energy was injected in all that India did. All pending projects and requests were processed faster and executed efficiently. The leadership in India kept Afghanistan under regular review and that had an electrifying effect."

Pakistan remains a bugbear for India. This sets the tone for T.C.A. Raghavan to reflect on India's policy options *vis-a-vis* Pakistan. Having served as India's High Commissioner in Islamabad, the author describes Pakistan as a "fortress". This, he writes, has "meant obviously a worldview and a mindset that is highly and excessively securitized, prone to thinking in terms of zero sum games, in which the geopolitical easily outweighs the geo economic and, finally, there is the inability to disaggregate the tactical from the strategic and the long term." While describing the 'engagement-disengagement' binary of India and Pakistan relations, the author states that the "challenge for our foreign policy and diplomacy with adversarial neighbours in the future will be to combine a securitized approach with a de-securitization agenda and seeking to expand the profile of de-securitization in India's overall policy profile."

In a different context, Lalitha Kumaramangalam delves into the role and significance of women in building a strong India and the fact that women continue to trust Modi. Indeed, in terms of sheer size and scale and reach, the Prime Minister has revolutionised the lives of millions of women. One example, she notes, is Modi's announcement in 2018 for permanent commissions for women officers selected through the Short Services Commission in the Armed Forces. Soon thereafter, the Defence Ministry announced in March 2019 that "women officers would be granted Permanent Commission in all ten branches of the army—truly a salute to the valour, dedication and resilience of Indian women." In a nuanced way, the author communicates that women are strong but more importantly how to change the way one perceives that strength.

Picking on the critical issue of the social media challenge to national security, Dhruv Katoch writes, "While a more open and democratic spread of information is a necessary component to informed decision making, it can also transform into a strategic weapon in the hands of terrorists, insurgent groups, anti-social elements or governments engaged in conflict". He suggests that there is a "need for information dominance which perhaps points to the requirement of the Prime Minister also having a National Information Advisor on the lines of the National Security Advisor".

The next two chapters are critically relevant and foremost in the minds of political leaders and security planners. As the Pakistan-China nexus grows stronger, India needs to calculate and prepare for implications including a two-front war, which India's military planners have feared for several decades. However, S.L. Narashimhan, an experienced hand on China, interestingly writes about confidence-building measures. He observes, "China is a big neighbour and cannot be wished away. The actions of China in the past several months along the LAC have resulted in strained relations. Unless the *status quo ante*—as existing before China mobilised its troops in 2020—is achieved, it will be difficult to keep the bilateral relations on an even keel. Unlike in the past when the boundary-related incidents were kept separate from the other parts of the relationship, this time such a separation is not possible."

Maroof Raza, in his chapter, strongly believes that India's Kashmir policy is inseparable to its Pakistan approach. He writes about the end of strategic restraint under Modi's leadership observing "In the past, all Pakistan-led and sponsored terror attacks across India and not just in Jammu & Kashmir had met with New Delhi's tepid response based on 'strategic restraint'." He then goes on to write that the *jihadi* terrorist attack on 18 September 2016 in Uri was a 'tipping point' and that the political leadership was "willing to respond and retaliate to Pakistan's cross-border violence".

In the final chapter, Ranjit Pachnanda writes about the disaster preparedness of India and the efforts undertaken by the NDA Government, especially PM Modi, to make India disaster resilient. He ends by citing PM Modi's attributes of stellar statesmanship and indomitable leadership by noting that "true leadership is not to make someone do something, but it is to make someone do something not because you want him to do it but because he wants to do it himself".

This volume provides an honest and comprehensive assessment by an eclectic mix of experts of the performance of the Modi government, which has now completed two years of its second term. We like to take the opportunity to thank each one of them and hope that readers will form their own objective views on reading it.

5 August 2021 **EDITORS**

1

Modi's Quest and Action for Securing India

Anirban Ganguly

In the summer of 2020, at the height of China's subversive manoeuvring along the border in Ladakh, over 72 per cent Indians clearly reposed their trust in Prime Minister Narendra Modi on matters of national security. They saw that Modi was firmly handling and responding to any attempts to make incursions into Indian territory. On 3 July 2020, Modi travelled to Nimu, 3,140 metres above sea level in the heights of Ladakh, to interact with soldiers and give a clear message to those who attempted to violate India's territorial integrity. He pointed out that 'India's commitment to peace must not be seen as India's weakness.'

This was a clear assertion that India does not stand any more on the crutches of a powerless philosophy of peace at any cost but is willing to defend and fortify its borders and all that is legitimately its. In the same historic address, Modi pointed out how the fortification of India's borders had gathered great momentum and there was increased allocation of resources to lay the foundations of a comprehensive and multi-dimensional border infrastructure. Prime Minister Modi always felt the need to initiate comprehensive steps in order to strengthen coordination between forces and thus give a major thrust towards the strengthening of national security. A long felt and needed overhaul of the Indian defence and security establishment was taken up when Modi announced the formation of the Chief of Defence Staff in his Independence Day Address on 15 August 2019. He said:

> *You must have noticed that deliberations are on since a long time to bring reforms in military infrastructure, armed forces and military resources. Previous governments have also discussed the same. Several commissions have been formed and all the reports have brought to light the same issues. There is hardly any difference, but this has been stated repeatedly. There indeed is coordination between our Navy, Army and Air Force. We can be proud of the arrangement of our armed forces. Any Hindustani can be proud of the Indian Military. They also strive for modernity in their own way. But the world is changing today and the scope of war is changing, the nature of war is also changing. It is becoming technology driven; in the circumstances India too should not have a fragmented approach. Our entire military power will have to work in unison and move forward. Things cannot move smoothly if anyone from the Navy, Army and Air Force is a step ahead of the other two forces, while the other two are lagging behind. All three should move simultaneously and at the same pace. There should be good coordination and it should be relevant with the hope and aspirations of our people. It should be in line with the changing war and security environment in the world and today I want to announce an important decision from Red Fort. Subject experts on the issue have been demanding this for a long time. Today we have decided that we will now have a Chief of Defence Staff (CDS) and after formation of this post all the three forces will get effective leadership at the top level. The CDS system is a very important and compelling task in our dream to reform the strategic pace of Hindustan in the world."*

Besides demonstrating his government's ability to respond, react and anticipate when it came to protecting India's security and strategic interests, this was another milestone move that demonstrated Modi's commitment and determination to push India's defence establishment and its national security paradigm to the next stage. The question that naturally arose was how come such a crucial game-changing reform was left unaddressed for so many decades; how was it that despite debating and discussing the need for such a reform, no government in the past, especially those that ruled India for over five decades and drew up most of its defence roadmaps always avoided addressing this issue.

Launching the *Seemant Vikas Utsav* [Border Development Festival] in November 2020, Union Home Minister Amit Shah, for instance, spoke of how the effort to develop India's borders was now comprehensive, time-bound and systematic. Shah gave out figures demonstrating the purposeful intervention that the Modi Government had made in enhancing and modernising India's borders:

> *"Between 2008 and 2014, the speed of re-surfacing of border roads was 170 kilometres, which has been increased by the Modi government from 170 kilometres to 480 kilometres.... From 2008 to 2014, 230 km of road cutting and formatting was being done annually along the Indo-China border; between 2014 and 2020 it was increased from 230 to 470 km. Only one tunnel was built between 2008 and 2014, and between 2014 and 2020 we have made six new tunnels and started work on 19. Between 2008 and 2014, a budget of Rs. 3,300 crore was allocated and during the Modi government the budget for 2017-18 was Rs. 5,400 crore which was increased to Rs. 6,700 crore in 2018-19 and in 2020-21 work of Rs. 11,800 crore has already been done."*

The aim of the *Seemant Vikas Utsav* was inspired by Prime Minister Modi's emphasis, since 2014, of strengthening India's borders and making them impregnable. The deeper objective was to create a border eco-system in which communities living along the border would be the principal beneficiaries of speedy all-round development while also becoming participants in keeping the areas secure. As Shah said, the aim was to:

> *"Bring good governance and development to border areas. Citizens living in border villages should get the same facility as citizens living in our cities. Along with this, the aim of the* Seemant Vikas Utsav *is to sensitize the population of these areas to the importance of national security and share the sensitivity of the security aspect and strategic importance of border areas."*

India's border policy, thus, has been drastically transformed in the last seven years. For decades after independence, successive Congress governments stuck to Nehru's philosophy of neglecting the borders in order to defend them. The Defence Minister in the Congress government, A.K. Antony, admitted as much in the Lok Sabha when he said, on 6 September 2013: 'The independent India had a policy for many years that the best defence is not to develop the border. Undeveloped borders are safer than developed borders. So, for many years, there was no construction of roads or airfields on the border areas..."

This then was the myopic approach to fortifying India's borders, an approach that was driven by a strange logic, by an apparent unwillingness to think in terms of achieving India's strategic objectives, long and short term. There were stalwarts who called for strengthening India's defence in the early years of independence. When Parliament discussed the international situation on December 6, 1950, two crucial figures made forceful and convincing interventions calling for the need to evolve a distinct defence policy and approach. With the war raging in the Korean peninsula, an increasingly aggressive Communist regime ensconced in China, a belligerent and predatory Pakistan on the Western front and armed Communist insurrectionists within the country, India was faced with a volatile strategic environment. Its defence imperatives had to be spelt out and its strategic objectives and plans needed to be worked out. Parliament had convened to debate these issues. Congress stalwart, later the founder of the Swatantra Party, N.G. Ranga, wanting to know the defence preparedness that India was working out and argued, for instance, that 'peace can be made sound, strong and stable only when we are in a position to make ourselves strong strategically as well as industrially...'

Dr. Syama Prasad Mookerjee, free India's first Industry Minister, who had a few months earlier, in April 1950, resigned from the Nehru cabinet, and had begun emerging as the rallying point for an opposition nucleus in Parliament, spoke presciently when he argued, that:

> *"The doctrine for which India has stood for has been the doctrine of live and let live. At the same time, if the danger signal comes, if the red signal comes, what is it that India will do? Suppose the Himalayas, which were considered to be impregnable, that huge border covering 2,000 miles for which no separate precaution or defence was thought to be necessary, but which has suddenly become an important frontier, happen to be the line*

> *through which there is penetration or infiltration into India, how is India going to defend herself? Today two things are vitally necessary. We have to strengthen our military position and if we cannot do it alone, we shall have to do it in collaboration with others with whom we can stand on a common platform in defence of a common ideology..."*

But Nehru stuck to displaying a strangely neglectful approach to India's defence. We can sample here a few more instances. Some time in 1955, Nehru was of the clear opinion that 'the proper way to consider defence is to begin to forget the military aspect. Defence is considered far too much in military terms', he lamented. Some time in 1958, when asked on the possibilities of aggression and India's defence preparedness, Nehru 'had asserted that the nation had the spirit to defend itself by *lathis* [sticks] and stones if need be; therefore, I am not afraid of anybody invading India from any quarter.' Thus, in Nehru's narrative of India's defence, sticks and stones were the ultimate arbiter of national defence. Over the decades, Nehru did not alter his attitude, until the 1962, Chinese invasion of India.

Replying to an intense discussion on a motion on India-China relations on 27 November 1959, Nehru poured scorn on Dr. Ram Subhag Singh, Congress Member of Parliament from Sasaram, Bihar, who had suggested that a proactive industrialisation drive be undertaken in NEFA and Ladakh regions. "Some suggestions made", said Nehru, rather surprised that he could be caustic against those who had foresight and spoke intelligently, "Dr. Ram Subhag Singh said that we should industrialise NEFA, the Ladakh area and—where else? It is a noble ambition of Dr. Ram Subhag Singh. But before we do that, we have to think of the little country of India also. We have to deal with and industrialise it. We might concentrate on industrialising India first before we go across the Himalayas for that purpose. It shows the enthusiasm of our honourable colleagues here in this Parliament, but it also shows that in their enthusiasm they sometimes overshoot the mark and that is not helpful."

Nehru's reply, thus, was astounding. Singh had made the right point; he was strategically prescient. Had the frontier areas and Ladakh seen a massive development drive, India's borders would have been secured long ago, and yet Nehru heckled him. What was also surprising was that he considered NEFA and Ladakh as separate from India and strangely spoke of concentrating on industrialising *India* first. Prolonged and unexplained neglect of India's Northeast also gave rise to crucial security challenges as well. Whether it was pushing defence indigenisation or creation of a chain of border roads, Nehru's predominant record was that of neglect by omission.

In Nehru's era, it was the Bharatiya Jana Sangh (BJS), political predecessor of the BJP, then nowhere near achieving the status of India's ruling party, that had spelt out the need for a strong defence policy and to strengthen India's defences. In its manifesto for the second general elections in 1957, the BJS, for instance, spoke of the need for a 'Defence Plan' and accorded it top priority, with Pandit Deendayal Upadhyaya, then General Secretary of the party, writing that the BJS 'proposed to augment the defence potential of the country by expanding, nationalising and modernising the armed forces.' It emphasised the need for compulsory military training of 'all young people' and had proposed the setting up of a 'Border Police Establishment under the Centre.' The BSF was eventually formed in 1965. The BJS also spoke on the need to modernise the intelligence department. In its poll manifesto for the third general election in 1962, Upadhyaya observed that the BJS, proposed to prepare 'a Defence Plan as part of the Five-Year Plan' and pledged to adequately augment the defence potential of the country 'with all modern weapons, missiles, submarines, fighters, etc.'; with weapons 'manufactured and/or procured without the country joining any military bloc.' The call of Upadhyaya and the BJS was to 'modernise the military'. With regard to the frontiers, Upadhyaya wrote in December 1961 that the 'policy should be of defending them and not discussing them...' The BJP in power, especially since, 2014, has displayed a clear adherence to that original doctrine as enunciated by the BJS under Upadhyaya. The Modi security doctrine is a practical implementation of the BJS's and later the BJP's security doctrine as articulated over the decades.

We have seen how the Modi security doctrine laid principal emphasis on the strengthening of India's border defence infrastructure.

In fact, the work was intensified in the last seven years. The Border Roads Organisation (BRO), for instance, has received a special fillip in its functioning; this includes a systematic increase in its budget in the last few years. To point out a few strategic achievements—the 'world's longest highway tunnel' the Atal Tunnel, inaugurated by Prime Minister Modi in October 2020, is a crucial lifeline to the border. ' Forty-four bridges of strategic importance in sensitive areas', near the Western, Northern and North Eastern border, covering seven states and UTs, were operationalised in October 2020 providing India with significant strategic advantage along the border in those sectors. In keeping with his vision of significantly enhancing India's indigenous defence production capabilities, the Modi government launched the Defence Acquisition Procedure 2020, which has a 'two-pronged approach towards indigenisation of defence equipment production.' It aims to 'provide an impetus to the growing domestic industry'. Under this policy, 'specific categories of goods were exclusively reserved for Indian vendors, with reward for those using indigenous raw material.'

In order to boost and support the creation of a domestic market, the Modi government clarified that 'it would be procuring goods worth Rs. 4 lakh crore domestically within the next five to seven years...' At the Commanders' Meet in March 2021, Modi stressed on the importance of 'Aatmanirbharta' in the 'national security architecture' and not just 'in sourcing equipment and weapons but also in various doctrines, procedures and customs practised in the armed forces.' In fact since 2014, this is the line of action that Modi has pursued.

These are the some of the outer manifestations of the essence of the Modi security doctrine. It is a doctrine that emerges from the fundamental belief that India's national security is non-negotiable, that its defence, security and freedom are not commodities and hence not to be bartered or diluted or compromised. This fundamental belief and conviction of 'India First' that Modi articulated early in his first term has defined and driven his global engagement and his pursuit of India's strategic interests.

Dr. Syama Prasad Mookerjee, himself a strong votary of India's defence indigenisation and preparedness, had once observed that:

> *"A nation must first be physically strong and adequately armed before it can proclaim and defend moral doctrines. That nation is truly great which has force and strength at its disposal but never abuses them for the advancement of self-interest or self-aggrandisement."*

The national security approach of Modi's 'New India' is in line with that articulation. India aspires to emerge as a leading power standing on solid foundations of a new security vision.

NOTES

Amiya Rao & B.G. Rao, *Six Thousand Days: Jawaharlal Nehru Prime Minister*, 1974.

Anirban Ganguly, 'How Nehruvian Consensus Compromised India's Security', *The Daily Guardian*, June 29, 2020.

Complete Works of Deendayal Upadhyaya, Vol. 10, 2019.

'Independence Day: Full text of PM Modi's address to nation' accessed at: https://www.businesstoday.in/latest/economy-politics/story/independence-day-pm-modi-address-nation-full-text-speech-15-august-red-fort-222154-2019-08-15

'Over 72 per cent trust PM Modi on matters of national security', *The Times of India*, June 24, 2020.

PM visits Nimu in Ladakh to interact with Indian troops: https://pib.gov.in/PressReleseDetail.aspx?PRID=1636130

'PM Modi stresses indigenisation of national security system at commanders' meet', *The Times of India*, March 6, 2021.

Parliamentary Debates, Official Report, 6 December, 1950 – Motion Regarding the International Situation.

Union Home Minister Shri Amit Shah addressed the Border Area Development Festival – 2020 programme at Dhordo (Kutch), Gujarat: https://pib.gov.in/Pressreleaseshare.aspx?PRID=1673175

2

Strategies to Countering Insurgency in Assam

Sarbananda Sonowal

The negligence of a few could easily send a ship to the bottom, but if it has the wholehearted cooperation of all on board, it can be safely brought to port. These words of Sardar Vallabhbhai Patel are a perfect analogy to describe the insurgency that wrought havoc in the socio-political and economic life of Assam during the last four decades *vis-a-vis* the present state of affairs.

In 1979, the State witnessed two major incidents, i.e., the emergence of the Assam movement led by the All Assam Students Union against illegal migration of Bangladeshi nationals and an armed uprising under the banner of the United Liberation Front of Assam (ULFA). Both the movements might apparently be different in their objectives but there were many common factors that stoked these movements.

The people of Assam for a long time had a strong feeling of alienation from mainland India. Apart from geographic remoteness, the feeling of alienation fuelled a strong emotional disconnect. There were other factors that contributed to disillusionment in the minds of the people. Most prominent among these was the utter neglect towards the North-East by successive Central governments since Independence. At the same time, the historical background of the trust deficit that prompted a secessionist movement in Assam cannot be overlooked.

In India's freedom movement, Assam played a very important role. But when the time for freedom from British rule inched closer, a very significant incident happened that cast a long-term impact on the future course of Assam's history. At the height of India's partition, the Cabinet Mission proffered the 'grouping scheme' which ran the risk of clubbing Assam with Bengal, presently known as Bangladesh. The central leadership of the Congress Party, going against the wishes of the people of Assam, sided with the proposal of the Cabinet Mission. At such a crucial time, Mahatma Gandhi stood by the side of the indigenous people of Assam. Gandhiji advised the provincial Congress led by Gopinath Bordoloi to wage a *satyagraha* against its high command as it tried to discard the people of Assam. Had it not been Gandhiji's support, the identity of the people of the North-East would have been totally different today. This incidence hurt Assamese sentiment deeply. It is ironical that the Congress governments in the last 70 years did almost nothing to heal this grievous wound. Instead, consistent negligent attitude of successive Congress governments gave a stimulus to the feeling of alienation.

For instance, the people of Assam in 1955-57 launched a massive movement against the Central Government's indifferent attitude towards their demand for establishment of an oil refinery in Assam. However, disregarding the potential of the State in the petroleum sector, the Congress Government at the Centre preferred to set up a refinery at Barauni in Bihar. Nevertheless, under strong public pressure and after prolonged agitation, Jawaharlal Nehru awarded a small refinery near Guwahati. The experience of the Refinery Movement made the people of Assam realise that the Central Government could be persuaded to fulfil their aspirations only through persistent struggle.

The 1962 India-China War further intensified the feeling of neglect in the minds of the Assamese people. The then Prime Minister's speech on All India Radio, after the fall of Bomdilla on November 20, 1962, saying that his heart went out to the people of Assam is still considered an example of his indifferent attitude towards the State.

Thus, decades of neglect and apathy by successive Central governments and lack of development prompted a feeling of alienation among the people of Assam and created an emotional disconnect with mainland India. In the absence of a strategic approach by earlier governments to realise the aspirations of the people, insurgency took root in Assam in 1979 with the rising of the ULFA. On the other hand, there had also been a plethora of grievances of various ethnic communities of Assam at being marginalised and denied an equal stake in the system by successive Congress governments ruling both at the Centre and in the state. The corollary of events and experience thereon widened the emotional divide and encouraged the disillusioned youth of several ethnic communities to float their own militant outfits which include the Bodo Liberation Tiger Forces (BLTF), National Democratic Front of Bodoland-Saoraigwra (NDFB), Karbi National Volunteers (KNV), Dima Halam Daoga (DHD), United Peoples' Democratic Solidarity (UPDS), Koch Rajbangshi Protection Force, Rabha National Security Force, etc. Apart from these, Assam-based militant outfits and a few other militant groups active in the bordering states, such as NSCN (K), NSCN (I-M), People's United Liberation Front (PULF) and National Liberation Front (BNLF) also set up base in Assam. All these outfits claimed to be working for protecting the interests of their respective communities. Their avowed goals range from protection of the interests of the 'natives' from foreign immigrants to formation of an autonomous district or state and creation of a separate state within the Indian Union to complete secession from it.

Till 2014, India dealt with various insurgent outfits primarily with a militaristic approach. But one cannot triumph over militancy solely or even primarily through military action alone. Instead of containing insurgency, such an approach can rather reinforce the resolve of the insurgence outfits. Without an understanding of the ideological roots that gave birth to militancy, restoring permanent peace in Assam was not possible. This implies that apart from military operations, the focus should have been on addressing the deep-rooted issues such as inclusive growth, generating employment opportunities and fulfilling ethnic aspirations within the mandate of the Indian Constitution. However, lack of a strategic approach by successive Central governments in dealing with militancy or rather the policy of 'wait and watch' with the hope that in course of time people's grievances and demands would wane actually backfired. This microscopic point of view of earlier governments worsened the situation as they failed to realise that ULFA and other militant outfits of Assam were driven more by a sense of 'neglect' rather than the absence of nationalist sentiment. The best way to overcome this is to undertake and implement appropriate economic reforms and development projects sensitive to the region's specific requirements apart from confidence-building and empowerment of local people as well as removing age-old isolation from mainland India.

However, the Central governments in the past, being oblivious of the real causes and their military response, aggrieved the people further and swelled the emotional divide. That is why perhaps even after several military operations like '*Operation* Bajrang' in 1990, '*Operation* Rhino' in 1991, '*Operation* All Clear' in 2003 and despite over 10,000 counter-insurgency operations with a death toll of over 5,000 militants during 23 years between 1990 and 2013, there had been little success in weaning youth off militancy. The ULFA still survived with a sizeable support base in rural Assam. In fact, a large section of the people of Assam considered the ULFA and other militant organisations as an answer to the anger and the frustration of the Assamese against the step-motherly attitude of Delhi. To put it succinctly, the bullet failed to contain insurgency in Assam; rather, it kept on distancing the people from the mainstream.

Considering the scale and depth of the seriousness of issues that plagued Assam and the Northeastern states, the country desperately needed a visionary leader who could risk everything for safeguarding and upholding the interests and aspirations of the people who are victims of perennial neglect and living in difficult conditions. At such a crucial juncture, the emergence of a dynamic leader like Prime Minister Narendra Modi, who has vast exposure of the Northeast, altogether changed the socio-political scenario in this region. The Prime Minister, with his deep understanding of Assam's cultural and political ethos, is well aware of the myriad problems including partition of the country and its effect on Assam's demography apart from transportation bottlenecks, economic backwardness, language movement and insurgency. It is his understanding about the causes of the trust deficit that moved the common people of the region not to lose hope in India's democracy and acted as a boon in dealing with insurgency in Assam.

After coming to power, Modiji listed out a well thought-out plan to give a healing touch pushing development to its zenith in the Northeast. During the last six years, his policy of inclusive growth, *"Sabka Saath, Sabka Vikas, Sabka Viswas"*, has played a magical role in building new confidence among the people, narrowing the emotional gap and building confidence. In his maiden speech in Parliament, the Prime Minister made his goal clear for development of the Northeast terming this region as the "New Engine of India's Growth" and the eight states as *'Astalakshmi'* of the country. He has adopted a focused approach to deal with the regional imbalance caused by the neglect and mis-governance of previous governments.

The Prime Minister took a series of steps to remove geographic isolation by taking up connectivity projects in a big way. If one goes by statistics, during the last seven decades, only three bridges were built over the Brahmaputra. But Modiji, in his first term as PM, increased it to six by expediting construction of three more bridges which had remained incomplete for several years. Today, the situation is such that as many as six more bridges over the Brahmaputra have been sanctioned, boosting connectivity immensely.

Today, the Indian Railways has touched every Northeastern states. During 2014-19, the Ministry of Railways managed to commission 231 new railway lines in the Northeastern states. Double-lining and electrification of railway lines in Assam is moving speedily under the NDA Government. The focus has been on the development of infrastructure and improved connectivity in this region to ensure that Assam and the other Northeastern states duly participate in the economic progress of the country. The average annual expenditure of laying new lines, gauge conversion and doubling infrastructure projects in the north-eastern region during 2014-19 was Rs. 26,022 crore per year as against only Rs. 11,527 crore per year during 2009-14.

Domestic and international air connectivity under the UDAAN scheme received a major boost with the construction of new and the renovation of existing airports as well as the launching of international flights. In the case of roads, nearly 27,000 km have been laid under various schemes in the region, out of which around 10,000 km were constructed in Assam alone. Besides, dredging of the Brahmaputra and Barak opened up new business opportunities.

The Prime Minister's sincerity for development of the Northeast and to bridge the emotional gap can be gauged from the fact that since assuming office, he has personally visited the region around 35 times. He has sent ministers and officers of the Central Government every 15 days to review and monitor implementation of important projects. This has led to speedy implementation of projects. It is having a real cascading effect on the development narrative and countering insurgency in the State.

Industrial growth is another area which was conspicuously neglected by the previous Central governments, thus limiting economic progress of the State. The tea industry thrived because it was owned mostly by private players. But in the public sector, there was no PSU worth mentioning except a few in the petroleum sector. Contrary to such a bleak record of the Congress Government, the NDA Government in last six years sanctioned more than Rs. 42,000 crore in the hydrocarbon sector alone. Besides, the present Central Government has taken steps for value addition in the existing refineries so that they become sustainable. As part of this, a bio-fuel plant is coming up at Numaligarh Refinery Limited, which is an offshoot of the Assam Accord. Further, under the *Pradhan Mantri Urja Ganga,* a 729-km long Barauni-Guwahati Natural Gas Pipeline (BGPL) is also being constructed which will provide availability of clean and eco-friendly fuel to the industrial, commercial, domestic and transport sectors to the Northeastern part of India. Bolstered by the Prime Minister's visionary leadership, the Assam Government organised Northeast

India's first ever Global Investors Summit under the tagline 'Advantage Assam, India's Expressway to the ASEAN' in February 2018 at Guwahati. The Summit resulted in the signing of 245 MOUs with an investment commitment amounting to approximately Rs. 79,000 crore by various investors.

Meanwhile, the Prime Minister has also taken a series of steps to ensure that the unique linguistic, cultural and social identity of Assam is adequately protected. Steps of this kind have not only brought the people of the region closer to mainland India but have also helped in establishing an economic equilibrium, which has a direct impact on countering insurgency.

As a result of the Central Government's efforts for mainstreaming the Assamese population, people's faith in the Government has increased manifold. Consequently, militancy has started to fizzle out fast. A strong feeling of nationalism is growing in the minds of the people. This is quite visible from the spontaneous participation of the people from all walks of life in the three-day celebrations of Independence Day and Republic Day which the State Government introduced after coming to power in 2016. With unprecedented infrastructural development, industrial growth, connectivity boost, economic empowerment and steps for safeguarding the unique identity, culture and rights of the Assamese people in the last six years, nationalism has become more vivid in Assam today than it has ever been before. This transformation of public sentiment has led to the erosion of the support base of various militant organisations of Assam.

Apart from the above, demonetisation was also a major reform which cut short terror funding that gravely affected the functioning of the insurgent outfits. After demonetisation, the outfits ran out of money and consequently suffered shortages of essential commodities and arms and ammunition. Many youth who were lured by monetary gain left the path of violence and many outfits were forced to join peace talks with the Government.

Moreover, most of the militant outfits of Assam used to operate from the soil of neighbouring countries. In order to tackle insurgency in Assam, a durable relationship with South-East Asia and the BBN countries (Bangladesh, Bhutan and Nepal) was of prime importance. In this context, the Prime Minister's 'Friendly Neighbourhood' and 'Act East Policy' have proved to be major diplomatic breakthroughs in dealing with insurgency in the Northeast. For instance, during last year alone, the armies of India and Myanmar launched two phases of joint operations along the Myanmar border targeting camps of insurgent groups operating in the Northeast. As a result of this military operation named 'Operation Sunrise', 63 cadres of different insurgent outfits including ULFA, NDFB and KLO surrendered to the police and security forces in Assam.

With regard to countering insurgency, the porous Indo-Bangladesh border had always been a serious cause of concern as it was also the gateway to cross-border terrorism. Though in the Assam Accord of 1985, complete sealing of Indo-Bangladesh border was agreed to be expeditiously executed, the successive Central governments did little to materialise this. However, the NDA Government, after coming to power in 2014, finalised the 'Land Swap' deal with the Bangladesh Government. As a result, border-sealing activities received fresh momentum. The Central Government has also introduced 'Smart Technology' to seal the border in the riverine areas which is expected to be completed soon and once and for all will stop illegal migration from Bangladesh and give a major boost to countering cross-border terrorism.

There is no doubt that the distrust caused by mis-governance and rampant corruption by successive state governments during the last seven decades also acted as a major gravitating force for the youth of the State to join insurgent outfits. Keeping this in view, when the BJP-led Government came to power in Assam in May 2016, it launched a full-scale war against corrupt practices in the government system. The anti-corruption drive has brought back people's confidence in the administrative machinery. This has not only helped the State Government to plug the loopholes in the administrative system and to do away with corruption but, more importantly, it has helped in accelerating the implementation of development projects. Moreover, the State Government's shift from traditional middlemen culture to beneficiary-oriented schemes has played an important role in economic empowerment of the people apart from countering insurgency. With better economic conditions, the youth in Assam today prefer to concentrate on constructive and positive things rather than becoming militants.

The State Government's policy of inclusiveness with committed efforts for protection of *Jati-Mati-Bheti* of the people living in the Barak and Brahmaputra valley and hills and plains have given a further boost to building a more cohesive Assamese society. All large and small communities in Assam today feel that their grievances are adequately addressed and political aspirations are equitably represented. This further eliminates the secessionist mentality from the minds of smaller communities.

Inspired by the Prime Minister's vision, the BJP-led State Government had also adopted a policy of zero tolerance towards terrorism. This zero tolerance attitude of the Central and State governments against terrorism has paid off well in dealing with insurgency. Relentless counter-insurgency operations have broken the backbone of militancy in the state. The fact is that since the state government came to power in May 2016, over 2,340 cadres belonging to various outfits such as ULFA, NDFB, KLO, RNLF, NSLA, NLFB, ADF and CPI (Maoist) have surrendered. The multipronged strategy adopted by the Government under the Unified Command Structure in the form of sustained counter-insurgency operations against active militant groups has paid rich dividends. This may be seen from the fact that the Guwahati Zoo Road grenade blast case of 2019 was solved by Assam Police in less than 48 hours when they arrested all the key accused.

Similarly, the dialogue processes continued by the Central Government with militant forces who were willing to join the mainstream immensely helped in countering insurgency. The dialogue processes led to almost all large and small insurgent outfits of the State including all factions of the NDFB and several other insurgent outfits to lay down their arms,. A new Bodo Peace Accord was signed bringing lasting peace to the region. The Central Government is also in a dialogue with the pro-talk faction of the ULFA. Further, the State Government has appealed to the ULFA (Independent) led by Paresh Baruah to come to the table for discussion.

Simultaneously, the Government has also taken up rehabilitation measures for the surrendered militants with all sincerity so that their assimilation into society becomes more seamless. Keeping this in view, the Government of India launched a revised Surrender-cum-Rehabilitation Scheme for NE militants through which, at present, the State Government is providing a stipend of Rs. 6,000 per month per cadre to 3,704 cadres belonging to ULFA, NDFB, KNLF, etc.

However, for rehabilitation and reintegration of the surrendered and Suspension of Operation (SoO) group cadres, who are not covered by the above scheme, the State Government has initiated a scheme called 'Swabalamban' since 2017-18 for imparting training to the former militants in order to help them to lead a productive life and merge meaningfully with society. Under this scheme, a skill developmental training programme was rolled out and so far a total of 1,800 have surrendered. The SoO cadres have been trained for developing entrepreneurship skills and out of them, 1,203 cadres have already been given financial aid of Rs. 1 lakh each—Rs. 50,000 as subsidy and the balance as a loan.

The last six years of the Narendra Modi Government have been an eye-opener for policy makers and strategists with regard to India's internal and external security. The Northeast which was once a cauldron of extremism, brings forth much learning before the world after the policy of 'inclusive growth' and 'healing touch' of the Prime Minister began to deliver results. Unequivocally, it is a milestone achievement for having restored normalcy in a region which otherwise hogged the headlines and drew attention for its troubles and conflicts. It is time to reflect on the learning more deeply and coherently so that the days of instability and insurgency never return to destabilise peace and prosperity in the Northeast.

3

Need for Police Reforms

Bibek Debroy

In any country, the primary responsibility of government is to protect the country against external aggression and ensure internal security and speedy dispute resolution. This is what our ancient texts called *raja dharma*, protection of property rights, punishing the wicked and protecting the virtuous. Since the end of the 18th century, we indiscriminately splice the words "law" and "order" and say the (internal) responsibility of the government is to ensure law and order. We don't differentiate between "law" and "order", which have different etymological roots. Perhaps any differentiation is difficult. One possibility is to interpret "law" as statutory law, which may not always be codified in a common law jurisdiction and interpret "order" as enforcement of that law. There are a large number of cases pending in India—62,000 in the Supreme Court, 4.5 million in the high courts and 34.9 million in the district and taluka courts. That doesn't make the deterrent aspect of *raja dharma* very credible. These are a combination of civil cases and criminal cases, with a relatively higher share of civil cases in high courts and a relatively higher share of criminal cases in district and taluka courts. For instance, out of the 34.9 million cases pending in the lower courts, 25.3 million are criminal cases and 9.6 million are civil cases.[1] When the expression "law and order" is used in popular parlance, one probably has in mind criminal justice rather than civil justice. Interpreted thus, "law" would mean the Indian Penal Code (IPC), Indian Evidence Act and Criminal Procedure Code (CrPC) and how courts enforce these, while "order" would mean how police enforce these. Semantics apart, criminal justice reform cannot be delinked from police reform.

Under the head of "police", the Home Ministry has three divisions—Police-I Division, Police-II Division and Police Modernisation Division. It is important to get this distinction out of the way, since the citizen's interface with the police and the discourse about police reform is usually about Police-I, not Police-II. Police-II means armed police—Border Security Force (BSF), Central Industrial Security Force (CISF), Central Reserve Police Force (CRPF), Indo Tibetan Border Police (ITBP), National Security Guard (NSG) and Sashastra Seema Bal (SSB). In contrast, Police-I means the civil police, though it is also true that State governments have increasingly resorted to Police-II to resolve law and order problems in their individual States.

Every year, the National Crime Records Bureau (NCRB) brings out a publication titled "Crime in India". This publication aggregates upwards data received from districts and States. The last such publication is for 2019. This is a rich source of data, including on custodial crimes and complaints against police personnel. Crimes are of two types, IPC and SLL.[2] In this wealth of data, let's focus on IPC crimes. They are representative. The charge-sheeting rate is defined as cases charge-sheeted divided by total cases disposed off. For something like murder, the all-India charge-sheeting rate is 85.3 per cent,[3] not quite the lackadaisical performance portrayed in depictions of the police in films and TV serials. But there are some catches. First, this varies across the type of crime. For something like auto or motor vehicle theft, it can be as low as 21.6 per cent. The citizen's perception of a public service is often based on minor crimes and not major ones. The annual ranking of public services by the Centre for Media Studies (CMS) is an example of this.[4] The police figure routinely and prominently in the list of public service providers where citizens experience, or perceive, corruption. With all the problems associated with such sample surveys, why do citizens bribe the police? The three most important cited reasons are getting a complaint/FIR registered, removing the name as an accused/witness and avoiding a challan for violation of traffic rules. As a side issue, bribery by the bribe-giver is not always undertaken with a desire to exercise one's rights. Bribery also occurs with a desire to prevent the law from taking its course. Second, as with other security agencies, the deterrence function of the police is not always visible. One does not realise, and therefore appreciate, crimes that have been prevented. Perceptions are formed on the basis of the motor vehicle theft issue that has not been addressed. As with many other government agencies, dissemination and public engagement by the police leaves a lot to be desired. Third, the charge-sheeting rate, as a metric, has total cases disposed off, as a denominator. It does not tell us anything about cases that are pending. What percentage of cases is still pending? Nearly 43.1 per cent of cases of murder are still pending investigation, underlining the supply-side constraints police face. Fourth, there is great variation in police performance across States. For instance, the all-India charge-sheeting rate is 72.7 per cent, masking a high of 95.1 per cent in Kerala and a low of 43.9 per cent in Haryana. Fifth, criminal justice delivery has to work through the court system and the usual delays in that also brush off on the police.

That diversity across police stations in different States, and even within States, is reflected in a laudable initiative undertaken by the Home Ministry. This is an annual ranking of police stations. We can skip the methodological details of the ranking, which splice NCRB data with sample surveys.[5] But a quote is necessary to explain the motivation behind the ranking. "Performance measurement is an essential exercise in any organisation for evaluation of service delivery and identification of techniques for improvement.... The Government of India has in the recent years utilised Performance Measurement to effectively generate a sense of competition amongst States through the Ease of Business Rankings and between cities through the *Swachh Survekshan*, etc. This has led to more effective public delivery of services and greater citizen satisfaction. The same principle needs to be extended to the police also.... This summarised report reflects the directions of the Hon'ble Prime Minister while addressing the DsGP during the 2015 Conference in Kutch, Gujarat. He had directed that parameters should be laid down for grading police stations and assessing their performance based on feedback.

While the expression "police reform" suggests dramatic changes, as this ranking demonstrates, many improvements are soft, requiring no significant budgetary expenditure. There are best practices like "(a) identification of a Pradhan in the market who acts as a SPOC (Single Point of Contact) for everyone to interact with police results in quick response time; (b) regular interaction of Beat constables with people raises satisfaction level and shortens the response time; (c) adoption of a system like *Saanjh Kendra* which involves mediation by non-police senior citizens prevents law and order situations; and (d) updated websites with details of local police officers and quick action on the on-line complaints".[6] Typically, a police station is divided into different beats and strengthening the beat constable system, removing the anonymity and distancing associated with the police, has often been mentioned in the police reform agenda. To state the obvious, the beat constable system has been diluted over time and for the system to be effective, a constable has to remain on the same beat for a prescribed minimum period of time.[7] The Second Administrative Reforms Commission also discussed the issue of police reforms and mentioned the beat constable system. "The system of the beat police which worked well in the past has fallen into disuse and in big cities patrolling is done mainly in vehicles. The beat police apart from giving a sense of security to the citizens was also an important source of information. The Commission feels that this system needs to be restored and strengthened."[8] Section 65 of the Kerala Police Act, 2011, explicitly recognizes this.[9] To return to the 2019 annual ranking, citizen feedback highlights soft skills, rather than hard budgetary expenditure.[10] For example, (a) Separate crime registration counters/centres away from police stations; (b) Citizen grievance mobile app for easy registration of complaints, grievances and suggestions; this indicates lack of awareness of existing applications; (c) Centralized call centre engaging non-police persons for handling the issues before they go to the police;

(d) Need to change police culture to that of service provider rather than a wielder of power and authority through appropriate training; (e) More focus on community policing; (f) Training for emergency response; (g) Need to shift the focus from the elite to the common man." Such rankings are also illuminating because they shift the focus away from perceptions about the police based in metros. In the 2019 rankings, the top ten police stations were: (1) Aberdeen (Andaman & Nicobar Islands); (2) Balasinor (Gujarat); (3) Ajk Burhanpur (Madhya Pradesh); (4) AWPS-Theni (Tamil Nadu); (5) Anini (Arunachal Pradesh); (6) Baba Haridas Nagar (Delhi); (7) Bakani (Rajasthan); (8) Choppadandi (Telangana); (9) Bicholim (Goa); and (10) Bargawa (Madhya Pradesh). This was the pattern in earlier years as well. These are often police stations one has not heard of and "reforms" are driven by an ASP, Deputy SP or SHO. The challenge is to delink them from individual-driven initiatives and make them systemic.

Expectation on the part of citizens for better public service delivery is understandable. That reflects demand. However, supply-side constraints often impede adequate responses and more often than not, citizens are not aware of the constraints police operate under. It is possible to cite data from Bureau of Police Research and Development (BPRD) to make this point.[11] However, the case becomes more convincing if an external source is cited. Hence, these examples are from an independent report.[12] While the intention is not to over-burden this essay with quotes, quotes make the illustrations more dramatic. Therefore, here are a few statements from this report and these are only meant to be illustrative, not exhaustive. There is much more in similar vein.

- "The police in India works at 77 per cent of its sanctioned strength, or just 3/4th of its required capacity."
- "Vacancies in the senior ranks are higher than vacancies at the constabulary ranks.... Police being a State subject, the roles, functions and duties at the different ranks vary across States. In general, however, as per the BPRD general guidelines, the personnel of ranks ASI and above are assigned the role of investigating officers (IOs) in cases. Therefore, a bulk of the crime investigation work, alongwith other

decision-making duties are performed by the officers in most States. This makes it crucial for the sanctioned positions of officers, already in much lower proportion than that of the constabulary, to be filled completely. The trend, however, is the reverse."

- "Over the last five years, on an average, only 6.4 per cent of the police force have been provided in-service training. Senior police officers are much more likely to receive in-service training than the constabulary-level personnel."
- Across the 22 States, 70 police stations do not have access to wireless devices, 214 police stations do not have access to telephones, and 24 police stations do not have access to either wireless or telephones."
- "On an average, the police stations in India have six computers per police station, but States like Assam and Bihar have an average of less than one computer per police station."
- "About 240 police stations across the 22 States have no access to vehicles.... This situation is further complicated by the fact that there are only a few State police establishments that have vehicles capable of handling emergencies.... Forty-six per cent personnel have frequently experienced situations where they needed a government vehicle but it was not available. Further, 41 per cent personnel have frequently been in situations where they could not reach a crime scene on time because of lack of staff."
- "Twelve per cent personnel reported that there is no provision for drinking water in their police stations, 18 per cent said there are no clean toilets, and 14 per cent said there is no provision for seating area for the public."
- "Police personnel work for 14 hours a day on an average, with about 80 per cent police personnel working for more than 8 hours a day. Except Nagaland, the average working hours of personnel is between 11 to 18 hours in all of the selected 21 states."
- "Nearly one in two personnel work overtime regularly, while eight out of ten personnel do not get paid for overtime work."
- "Nearly three out of five respondents from the families of

personnel were dissatisfied with the government provided housing quarters."

- "One out of two personnel do not get any weekly off days."
- "More than half of the family members of the police personnel responded that in the past 2–3 years, their families (including police personnel) have not been on a leisure holiday. About 40 per cent reported not having visited relatives out of town and more than two-thirds of the respondents among family members responded that they have not gone for a religious pilgrimage in the past 2–3 years."
- "Three out of four personnel believe that their workload is affecting their physical and mental health.... More than 60 per cent of the respondents among the family members agreed with the statement that as compared to others, police officers are more prone to getting angry and irritable more easily and that police officers suffer more from mental health issues. About one third of the family respondents also agreed with the statement that as compared to others, police officers behave more badly with family, and are more prone to alcoholism."
- "One out of four personnel reported that senior police personnel ask their juniors to do their household/personal jobs even though they are not meant to do it."
- "Twenty-eight per cent police personnel believe that pressure from politicians is the biggest hindrance in crime investigation. One in three personnel have very frequently experienced political pressure in the course of crime investigation. Thirty-eight per cent personnel reported always facing pressure from politicians in cases of crime involving influential persons. Three out of five personnel reported transfer as the most common consequence of not complying with such external pressures."

These kinds of facts are a reality check on "police reforms". As mentioned earlier, the Home Ministry has a Police Modernisation Division. There is also a Union Government scheme to assist States in modernisation of police forces, the antecedents of which go back to

1969-70. On police reforms, the Home Ministry succinctly states, "Police reforms has been on the agenda of governments almost since Independence but even after more than 50 years, the police is seen as selectively efficient, unsympathetic to the under privileged. It is further accused of politicization and criminalization. In this regard, one needs to note that the basic framework for policing in India was made way back in 1861, with little changes thereafter, whereas society has undergone dramatic changes, especially in the post-Independence times.... "Police" being a State subject in the Seventh Schedule to the Constitution of India, it is primarily the State governments that have to implement the various police reforms/measures.... Various committees/commissions in the past have made a number of important recommendations regarding police reforms. Notable amongst these are those made by the National Police Commission (1978-82); the Padmanabhaiah Committee on restructuring of Police (2000); and the Malimath Committee on reforms in Criminal Justice System (2002-03). Yet another committee, headed by Shri Ribeiro, was constituted in 1998, on the directions of the Supreme Court of India, to review action taken by the Central Government/State governments/UT Administrations in this regard, and to suggest ways and means for implementing the pending recommendations of the above Commission."[13]

This quote gives us the bare bones on police reform issues. The roots go back to the pre-Independence days and to a Commission set up, just before 1857, to probe allegations of police torture in Madras Presidency.[14] Subsequently, in 1860, there was a Police Commission which drafted what became the Police Act of 1861, the basic statute that still governs the police. There was an Indian Police Commission in 1902-03, referred to as the first Police Commission, though it was really the second. After Independence, we had (1) A Police Reforms Committee in Kerala in 1959; (2) A series of Police Commissions in different States in the 1960s and 1970s (West Bengal in 1960-61, Punjab in 1961-62, Delhi in 1968, Tamil Nadu in 1971); (3) A Working Group on Police was set up by the First Administrative Reforms Commission in 1966; (4) the 1971 Gore Committee on Police Training; (5) the National Police Commission of 1977-81;[15] (6) the famous Prakash Singh case in

1996; (7) the Supreme Court directed the Ribeiro Committee in 1998; (8) the Padmanabhaiah Committee in 1980; and (9) the Malimath Committee (on criminal justice) between 2000 and 2003. As a result of the Prakash Singh case, the Supreme Court passed a judgement with directions for the Union Government and State governments. There was a new Model Police Act in 2006, which became a Model Police Bill in 2015.

This essay is not the place to review in detail the state of compliance, or non-compliance, by States with the Supreme Court directives. Suffice to say, "States were required to comply with the directives immediately, even if they were in the process of drafting their new Police Bills that, once enacted, would include the previous recommendations and replace the directives. In the short term, there was a lot of variation in the compliance by different states. Some states, such as Sikkim, Manipur, Meghalaya, Mizoram and Tripura took early steps to comply with all of the reforms. Partial compliance was reported by states such as Himachal Pradesh and Jharkhand. The majority, however, either sought to delay because they were in the process of drafting the Police Bills, sought to delay without giving a reason or expressed resistance and requested the Supreme Court to reconsider its decision."[16]

What's relevant for this essay is the Constitution and the Seventh Schedule. In the Seventh Schedule, public order (Entry 1) and police (Entry 2) are squarely in the State list. The present Constitution has been amended several times and is no longer the Constitution enacted in 1950. The 1950 Constitution was based on the Government of India Act of 1935 and even the Government of India Act of 1919. As a country's socio-economic and political conditions evolve, the dynamics of Union-State relations also change and need not be bogged down by what was historically relevant. With a transformation in the nature of "crime", isn't there a clear case for moving "police" to the Concurrent List, so that the entire country has a unified approach towards police and the handling of crime? Shouldn't there be a unified Police Act for the entire country? Under Article 252 of the Constitution, all this requires is the support of two or more State Legislatures and in no way does this undermine the rights of the States.

NOTES

1. https://njdg.ecourts.gov.in/njdgnew/?p=main/pend_dashboard Around 53,000 criminal cases have been pending for more than 30 years and around 317,000 have been pending for between 20 and 30 years.
2. SLL means special and local laws. Examples are laws against dowry, immortal trafficking, abuse of children, atrocities against SCs/STs and Arms Act.
3. These figures are from *Crime in India 2019*, Volume III, National Crime Records Bureau, https://ncrb.gov.in/sites/default/files/CII%202019%20Volume%201.pdf
4. *India Corruption Study 2018*, Centre for Media Studies, 2018, https://www.im4change.org/siteadmin/tinymce/uploaded/India%20Corruption%20Study%202018%20by%20CMS.pdf
5. See *Ranking of Police Stations 2019*, Ministry of Home Affairs, https://www.mha.gov.in/sites/default/files/RankingofPoliceSation_06122019E_0.pdf
6. Ibid.
7. In addition to the beat constable, the role of the Station House Officer (SHO) has also been diluted. The dilution had the desirable effect of diluting any local negative nexus, but it also diluted the positive benefits from the link.
8. *Fifth Report of Second Administrative Reforms Commission on Public Order*, 2007, https://darpg.gov.in/sites/default/files/public_order5.pdf
9. https://keralapolice.gov.in/storage/pages/custom/table/table-juypdtUu3picselajUlPVLZ76.pdf
10. Ibid.
11. Such as the publication titled *Data on Police Organizations.*
12. *Status of Policing in India Report 2019, Police Adequacy and Working Conditions*, Common Cause and Centre for the Study of Developing Societies, 2019, https://www.commoncause.in/uploadimage/page/Status_of_Policing_in_India_Report_2019_by_Common_Cause_and_CSDS.pdf
13. https://www.mha.gov.in/sites/default/files/PoliceReforms%28E%29181013.pdf.
14. The Torture Commission of 1855.
15. The difference in dates with the dates given in the quote above is explained by a difference between formation of a Commission and the submission of its report and placement in Parliament.
16. *Moving the Needle on Police Reforms, Why Reforms have Stalled and How to Make Progress*, Shruti Lakhtakia, Indian Police Foundation, 2020, https://www.policefoundationindia.org/images/resources/pdf/Shruti_Lakhtakia_Monograph_.pdf

4

Modi Government's War Against the Underworld

Satya Pal Singh

The word 'underworld' is not a legal connotation. In the world of crime, it is common parlance for an organised crime syndicate (or criminal gang) that is run in a hierarchical and dictatorial manner wherein, the top bosses and higher echelons of leadership remain insulated and cut off from the actual perpetrators of crime. These 'dons' live in a sordid world of secret communication with their loyal foot soldiers who, in turn, have their own minions to work for them. Loyalty is the most important consideration for entering such a network and betrayal is severely punished, more often than not with death. Such an organised crime network would include any unlawful activity by an individual or group, either as a member of an organised crime syndicate or on behalf of such a syndicate; by use of violence or threat of violence, or intimidation or coercion, or other unlawful means, with the objective of gaining pecuniary benefits or gaining undue economic or other advantages for themselves or any other person or group.

Organised crime has always existed in India in some form or the other. The core of organised crime activity is the supply of illegal goods and services to interested parties at an asked-for price. In India, the underworld, in addition to its traditional domains of criminal activities which include extortion, seeking protection money, contract killing, bootlegging, gambling, prostitution and smuggling, has now become deeply entrenched in narcotics, drug trafficking, illicit arms trading, *hawala*, money laundering and piracy of films and music. Their operations have become increasingly sophisticated and clandestine, and though it may be possible to have the actual perpetrators of crime arrested, prosecuted and even convicted; it is increasingly difficult to go beyond them in the hierarchy because of the provisions of the Indian Evidence Act. In the absence of a law like the Maharashtra Control of Organised Crime Act (MCOCA), confessional statements made before the police by criminals are inadmissible. People generally do not come forward to depose against hardened criminals and this becomes near impossible if the criminal hails from any underworld gang. India still lacks a good law for witness protection despite repeated demands from all quarters. Matters become much worse when the underworld gets entrenched in the legitimate businesses of a country as well. By employing illegitimate methods like monopolisation, terrorism, extortion and tax-evasion, they drive out lawful ownership and leadership of labour unions and extract illegal profits from the public. The underworld operatives are able to achieve this by corrupting public officials, especially the police, Home Department, Revenue Department, municipal corporations, prisons and courts to avert government interference. Even though rural India is not immune to this, it is essentially an urban phenomenon.

Police and the Public Order are State subjects under the 7th Schedule of the Constitution of India and, therefore, State governments are primarily responsible for the control of crime and the maintenance of public order in their jurisdictions. However, the Government of India not only supplements the efforts of the State governments but actively coordinates between two or more State governments and in a few specific areas takes direct action through its central agencies like the CBI, NIA, NCB and ED which have national jurisdictions. In the national capital, Delhi, and in all the Union Territories, the MHA directly administers policing issues. Subjects like terrorism, left-wing extremism, underworld, human trafficking, drugs, narcotics and arms and explosives, fake Indian currency notes (FICN), and issues of national security bear a substantial stamp of the Centre's involvement. The MHA provides financial assistance for modernisation of state police forces in terms of weaponry, communication, equipment, mobility, training and infrastructure. The MHA, besides administering the National Investigation Agency, responsible for investigating terror-related cases, runs the anti-narcotics operations through the Narcotics Control Bureau. The Ministry of Finance administers the Enforcement Directorate which is responsible for enforcing economic laws and fighting economic crimes like *hawala* and others. The Ministry of Personnel and Training is the administrative ministry for the Central Bureau of Investigation which investigates an array of offences ranging from special traditional crime to the underworld, from banking and financial frauds to wide-ranging corruption cases mainly under Central Government establishments. Therefore, we can say that the Union Government has the onerous responsibility of maintaining the internal security apparatus in the country.

The Modi Government came to power in 2014 riding on an anti-corruption, counter-terror, nationalism and development plank. In fact, the BJP from its inception in 1980 and also in its earlier avatar of the *Bharatiya Jana Sangh*, has always stood for clean and decisive governance. Prime Minister Modi was aware about the extent and depredations of the underworld and how its nexus with politicians and bureaucrats was eroding the developmental climate of India. The Centre and the BJP-led State governments have taken various stringent measures to tackle the menace of the underworld, especially in cities, by enacting tough laws and simultaneously strengthening the police and intelligence agencies. The Sub-Committee of the Chief Ministers on rationalisation of Centrally Sponsored Schemes, constituted under the chairmanship of Shivraj Singh Chauhan, the Chief Minister of Madhya Pradesh, recommended in 2015 that the schemes of 'Law and Order' and 'Justice Delivery System' be treated as part of the core National Development Agenda. The Modi Government accepted this recommendation and in pursuant of that, the NITI Aayog included the umbrella scheme of Modernisation of Police Forces (MPF) as a core scheme on 17 August, 2016. This scheme was approved by the

Government on 27 September, 2017, for implementation and funding the State/UT governments.

The Prime Minister, being well aware of the intricacies and inadequacies of the police system, in his first year in 2014, conceptualised the SMART model for policing. Modi, conscious of the fact that to effectively maintain the internal security of the country, meet the challenge of organised crime syndicates and to give a responsive welfare-oriented policing system in India, the whole police system required a complete overhaul. He gave a seminal concept, a *mool mantra* of sorts, which he himself named SMART police. This is an abbreviated form for S—Strict and Sensitive; M—Modern and Mobile; A—Alert and Accountable; R—Reliable and Responsive and T—Techno-savvy and Trained. To realise this concept on the ground, besides enhancing budgets for MPF, a clear and unalloyed message was sent across that there will be zero tolerance for terrorism, underworld and anti-national activities as well as for the creation and stashing of black money. This resolve to combat organised crime effectively is being implemented mainly by the CBI. This premier investigation agency plays a lead role in the war against national and transnational organised crime based on time-tested professionalism, transparency and the use of the latest scientific and investigative tools. The CBI undertakes investigation and prosecution of cases dealing with organised crime of a conventional nature having inter-state and international ramifications. Upon ratification of the United Nations Convention on Transnational Organised Crime (UNCTOC) by India, the Ministry of Home Affairs (MHA) designated the CBI to act as a nodal authority to receive and respond to all requests for assistance as a single point of reference and to act as a liaison between the Ministry of External Affairs (MEA) and other countries on matters relating to UNCTOC as well as the supplementary protocols thereto.

Laws against Underworld

There is no central legislation to suppress gang activity or underworld operations having country-wide applicability. Uttar Pradesh, the most populous and politically most powerful, has enacted the Uttar Pradesh Gangsters and Anti-Social Activities (Prevention) Act, 1986 which is applicable in that state only. In the 1990s, Mumbai city had become increasingly unsafe because of the depredations of 4-5 underworld gangs (mainly Dawood, Chhota Rajan, Arun Gavli, Amar Naik). The normal criminal laws were not effective to control the menace of the underworld as the criminal justice system had almost been crippled. Then the Shiv Sena and the BJP Government were ruling Maharashtra and with the persuasion of the police leadership, a stringent anti-gangster law in the name and style of MCOCA, 1999 was enacted by the Government. The same law was adopted by the Delhi Government. The Haryana Government has adopted the Haryana Control of Organised Crime Act (HCOCA) in August, 2019 almost verbatim to deal with gangsters and underworld. Apart from Maharashtra, Haryana and Delhi, the other states that have adopted this Act are Gujarat, Uttar Pradesh, Karnataka and Andhra Pradesh. These states, however, have their own versions of the law.

Attack on Black Money

After coming to power, the Modi Government, staying true to the BJP manifesto, in its first cabinet meeting on 27 May 2014 took a decision to form an SIT (Special Investigation Team) for probing black money cases and to bring back black money stashed abroad as per the Supreme Court of India's orders which was given in 2011. A committee was formed under Justice M. B. Shah to head the probing and a deputy governor of the RBI, CBDT Chairman, Revenue Secretary, the Directors of the IB and the CBI were made the members of this SIT. The SIT was also tasked to recommend amendments to existing laws or enact new laws and also to proactively engage with foreign governments to facilitate information-sharing on black money.

Resultantly, the Black Money (Undisclosed Foreign Income and Assets) and Imposition of Tax Act, 2015 was passed by Parliament in May, 2015 to curb black money or undisclosed foreign assets and income and imposed a tax and penalty on such income. The law was made effective from 1 July, 2015. The civil and criminal liabilities for holding black money were made stringent including rigorous imprisonment.

The Centre, in November, 2015, took an initiative to form a regional platform with South Asian countries for information-sharing on transnational organised crime. The delegates of seven countries—India, Bhutan, Nepal, Bangladesh, Maldives, Sri Lanka and Myanmar—in a conference held in New Delhi discussed the modalities for the creation of a regional hub for information and intelligence-sharing to enable all-member states to quickly respond to transnational organised crimes. The South Asia region was lacking such regional coordination mechanisms unlike Central Asia to facilitate criminal intelligence-sharing and operational coordination related to organised crime, including drug trafficking and money laundering. Earlier in the month, the Revenue Department of the Ministry of Finance hosted a three-day international meet 'Networking the Networks' from November 2 to 4, 2015, in New Delhi. The theme of the conference was 'Countering Illicit Financial Flows' originating from organised crime.

It was known that many tax evaders and underworld operatives were sending their ill-gotten money to Mauritius and getting it back as business money through money laundering. In 2016, India amended its Double Taxation Avoidance Agreement (DTAA) with Mauritius to plug certain loopholes. Now, a Mauritian entity will have to pay capital gains tax while selling shares in a company in India from April 2017. Earlier, the company could avoid tax as it was not a 'resident' in India. It could get away from the taxman in Mauritius too, due to non-taxation of capital gain for its residents . As a result, many shell entities sprang up in Mauritius to profit from investments in India and get away without paying taxes anywhere. Subsequently, India made and reviewed its DTAAs with more than 80 countries.

On 8 November, 2016, Modi took the country by surprise by announcing demonetisation of big currency notes of Rs. 1,000 and Rs. 500 to give a blow to black money hoarders and break the chain of black economy in the country. The Centre has also been successful in pressurising and convincing many countries, including Switzerland and other tax havens, for exchange of information regarding bank accounts maintained by many Indians. India entered into an agreement with Switzerland's Federal Tax Administration in 2018 for automatic information exchange, a major milestone in the Government's fight against black money stashed abroad.

Crackdown on Nexus

The Modi Government has compulsorily retired many officers from public service, especially in the Income Tax and Customs, who were accused of corruption, misuse of official position and other malpractices including their nexus with smugglers and the underworld. The Government has retired more than 100 senior officers, some of them even of the rank of Secretary under Fundamental Rules 56(j). The events that have unfolded in the last six years have not happened in the last six decades. The Prime Minister had declared from the ramparts of the Red Fort that no black sheep in the public administration will be tolerated. Many State governments have also taken stringent action against their erring officials who were found having a nexus with criminal and anti-social elements. After the serial bomb blasts in Mumbai in March 1993, it was widely believed, and also came on record, that some officials in the police, revenue, customs and income tax departments were directly and indirectly colluding with underworld elements. Some politicians were also accused of having a nexus with Dawood gangs.

In fact, the MHA had constituted a committee under the chairmanship of N.N. Vohra, which had gone into the nexus between the underworld and bureaucrats, the police and politicians. But unfortunately, this report was never made public despite the directions of the Supreme Court of India. However, the statement of the then Minister of Home Affairs (Shri Inderjeet Gupta) underlines the dreadful situation the country was facing. He had said, "There is nothing we can do to end the unholy nexus between criminals and politicians, politicians and bureaucrats. All we can do is to pass legislation which cannot be implemented. I see no end to the problems in the country, especially as there are criminals in every section of society". However, the Modi Government effectively broke this helplessness and the policy paralysis which was ailing the earlier governments. He had come with a resolute mind to break the nexus and gave a clear message that no person, however, important, was pardonable. He advocated zero tolerance towards these mites eating into the very system they are mandated to serve.

Actions against Underworld Dons

Since the Modi Government took over, a strong message was given to the underworld and terrorist organisations and their mentors that India was in strong and stable hands and no onslaught on its internal security as well as economic stability would be tolerated. Very early in its first term, the Government reiterated that it was committed to bringing back underworld dons Dawood, Chhota Rajan and other fugitives, to face the laws of the land.

After being on the run for the past 27 years, Chhota Rajan (Rajendra Sadashiv Nikalje alias Nana alias Seth alias Sir) was deported from Indonesia in November, 2015 by a joint team headed by CBI officials for facing trial in over 70 cases of murder, extortion and drug smuggling against him in Delhi and Mumbai. Ravi Pujari, running his own independent gang for more than 20 years and wanted in over 100 cases in various parts of the country, mainly in Mumbai and Karnataka, and who had remained a fugitive for about 15 years was ultimately tracked down in South Africa and deported to India in February 2020. Ravi was earlier a member of the Dawood gang but later shifted his loyalty to Chhota Rajan for a few years before operating independently from 2006.

Ejaj Lakdawala, a former associate of the Dawood Ibrahim and Chhota Rajan gangs at different times, had escaped from Nashik Jail in 1998 and was fugitive since then. He was believed to be operating from somewhere in North America and later frequently changing his locations in Southeast Asian countries. He was wanted in 27 cases of murder and attempt to murder and in 80 cases of threatening businessmen for extortion in Mumbai alone. He was ultimately arrested in January 2020 from Patna airport. Dawood Ibrahim has headed undoubtedly the biggest underworld gang in Southeast Asia and has been a fugitive for more than 30 years. He is a key conspirator of the 1993 serial blasts in Mumbai. The Modi Government has made its intentions clear that Dawood would be brought back to India to face the law. The Government tried to put pressure on Pakistan to extradite Dawood but it never acknowledged even his presence on its land. India's Permanent Representative to the UN, Syed Akbaruddin, had told the UN Security Council in July, 2019 that Dawood Ibrahim's illegitimate activities from a 'safe haven' that refuses to acknowledge even his existence pose a real danger. The D-Company criminals are joining hands with terrorists and are providing services such as counterfeiting, illicit financing, arms dealing, drug trafficking and smuggling terrorists across borders. On the other hand, terrorist organisations are increasingly involved in lucrative criminal activities such as trading in natural resources and human trafficking to raise funds. Akbaruddin mentioned that there are linkages between international terrorism and organised crime and it poses threats to international peace and security. As the world becomes more interconnected, these menacing networks are becoming increasingly intertwined.

India provided a dossier to the UAE about Dawood's properties including a company 'Golden Box' run by Anis Ibrahim, younger brother of Dawood. Besides Dubai, Dawood has investments in Morocco, Spain, UAE, Singapore, Thailand, Cyprus, Turkey, India, Pakistan and the United Kingdom. After the details provided by India, the UAE Government has seized the properties of Dawood assets worth Rs. 15,000 crore. This has been the biggest-ever crackdown on Dawood. The list of properties was provided to the UAE Government with a request to seize them in 2016 when Modi had visited the UAE.

Because of the recent upswing in cooperation between India and the UAE, Dubai is no longer a safe haven for Indian fugitives. The UAE, which had given shelter to Dawood for years, has extradited four high-profile gangsters during 2018. Farooq Takla, Dawood's aide, was also deported in March, 2018. Before that, in 2016, Abdul Wahid Siddibapa, associated with Indian Mujahideen, was extradited. The UAE's envoy to India credited important strategic ties and the personal touch between the leadership of the two countries.

Land border and Coastal Security

To contain and control cross-border crime, especially the smuggling of goods, cattle and persons, is also equally important from an internal security point of view. The underworld gangs mainly operate along the Indo-Nepal (1,751-km), Indo-Myanmar (1,643-km) and Indo-Bangladesh (4,156-km) international borders. The Centre has recently approved the construction and upgradation of 1,377 km long roads along the Indo-Nepal border. The Indo-Myanmar border is being effectively monitored by Assam Rifles to stop smuggling, especially of drugs. Before 2014, cattle smuggling was a menace and a big drain on national animal husbandry, mainly cows. In fact, the economy of Bangladesh was getting a big boost because of India's cattle trade. Beef and leather, which were being exported by Bangladesh, has now been effectively controlled. The Indo-Bangladesh border fencing work has almost been completed except for some riverine tracts.

Plenty of smuggling takes place over the sea and our coastline. We know the background of how the explosives and sophisticated arms and ammunitions were smuggled into Maharashtra through the Rajgarh coast before the 1993 serial blasts in Mumbai city. India has a coastline of 7,517 km and it is a major challenge before the law enforcement agencies to make it foolproof. However, the Government has made concerted efforts to mount surveillance on the sea. Fishermen have been provided now with biometric identity cards. All sea-going vessels above 20 metres length are mandatorily required to be fitted with an Automatic Identification System. Recently, as per the directions of the National Committee on Strengthening Maritime and Coastal Security, the Indian Space Research Organisation has been asked to provide 500 satellite-based transponders each to the more sensitive coastal states of Gujarat and Tamil Nadu. The Government has been effectively monitoring the coordination between the Navy, Indian Coast Guard and the Coastal Police of the coastal states. Much of the funding for coastal security comes from the Centre.

Human Trafficking

Human trafficking is a highly organised and lucrative crime and underworld syndicates are deeply entrenched in it. India recognises that human trafficking is a grave crime and is making continuous and concerted efforts to curb it. The MHA has been supplementing the efforts of the states by releasing funds for setting up Anti-Human Trafficking Units (AHTUs) in 50 per cent of the districts in all states. Recently, the Centre took a decision to establish AHTUs in all districts of states and UTs and also establish AHTUs under the para-military forces such as the BSF and SSB in border areas to check and curb transnational trafficking. Funds were released in March, 2020 for equipping offices and providing mobility.

The MHA holds meetings of nodal officers of AHTUs and other concerned agencies and coordinates with the Ministry of Women & Child Development (concerned with the issues of rehabilitation of victims of human trafficking), with the Ministry of Labour & Employment (that is concerned with placement agencies, etc.), Ministry of External Affairs (Protector of Emigrants) and the BSF and SSB who manage the international borders of neighbouring countries. The MHA provides guidance and advice to states and UTs through various advisories on measures to be adopted for handling human trafficking related issues.

Global Engagement on Cross-border Trafficking

India ratified the UNCTOC in 2011 and its Protocols: (i) Protocol to Prevent, Suppress and Punish Trafficking in Persons, especially Women and Children, and (ii) Protocol against the Smuggling of Migrants by Land, Sea and Air. India has signed a bilateral Memorandum of Understanding for Prevention of Human Trafficking with Bangladesh on 6 June 2015. A Joint Task Force of officials of the two countries has been constituted to periodically review the actions and initiatives required to contain human trafficking. An MoU has also been reached with the UAE on cooperation in prevention and combating human trafficking on 25 January 2017. It is aimed to enhance bilateral cooperation on issues of prevention, rescue, recovery, and repatriation related to human trafficking, especially of women and children, expeditiously. Likewise, a bilateral MoU on Human Trafficking has been signed with Cambodia on 27 January, 2018 and with Myanmar on 27 February, 2020.

Training is provided to state police personnel in prevention and investigation of human trafficking in partnership with BRP&D, UNODC, BSF, etc. This aims at capacity building of law enforcement agencies and generating awareness among them. India has also signed the SAARC Convention on Prevention and Combating Trafficking in Women and Children in Prostitution in 2002. To implement the objectives of the SAARC Convention, a Regional Task Force (RTF) has been constituted.

Child Protection Services Schemes to provide institutional and non-institutional care including 24x7 Child Helpline (Childline 1098) has been established by the Ministry of Women and Child Development. A national-level single Emergency Response Number 112 and app with 'Shout' facility for women in distress has been launched. India is amongst the few countries in the world with a National Database on Sexual Offenders. A national-level communication platform, Crime Multi Agency Centre (Cri-MAC), was launched by the MHA on 12 March 2020 facilitating dissemination of information about significant crimes including human trafficking cases across the country on real-time basis and enabling inter-State coordination. The Cri-MAC can *inter-alia* help in locating and identifying trafficked victims as also in prevention, detection and investigation of crimes.

Curbing Drug Abuse and Trafficking

Smuggling of narcotic drugs is the highest profit-making enterprise in the world. In recent times, it has become highly sophisticated. India's approach towards Narcotic Drugs and Psychotropic Substances (NDPS) is enshrined in Article 47 of the Constitution which mandates that the 'State shall endeavour to bring about prohibition of the consumption except for medicinal purposes of intoxicating drinks and of drugs which are injurious to health'. The NDPS Act, 1985 was framed taking into account India's obligations under the three UN Drug Conventions as well as Article 47 of the Constitution. This Act prohibits, except for medical or scientific purposes, the manufacture, production, trade, use, etc., of narcotic drugs and psychotropic substances.

India's initiatives since 2014 have largely been driven by the vision of the Prime Minister. While speaking in the *Mann ki Baat* episode on drug issues in December 2014, the PM referred to the drug menace as a complex 3D problem causing "Darkness, Destruction and Devastation". On the one hand, it is a psycho-social-medical problem with regard to the victim of drug abuse and, on the other, in so far as drug trafficking is concerned, the same is a criminal activity which has a close nexus with terrorism and other organised crime. Consequently, society, government and law all need to work together to confront this menace. Subsequently, speaking on the launch of the campaign for *Drug Free India* in February 2019, the PM emphasised the several steps taken by the Government to curb the illegal drug trade, especially drug trafficking across the border.

The NDA Government has placed the drug problem as a top priority that needs to be addressed from multiple perspectives. Accordingly, various ministries dealing with different aspects of drug control have put in place various programmes, plans of action and other measures to address the issue. Effective measures have been taken at the enforcement level, policy level, demand reduction level and strengthening the legal framework. Some of the major steps brought out are as follows:

Constitution of Narco Co-ordination Centre (NCORD)

NCORD was created on the recommendation of the National Security Adviser (NSA) in order to have effective coordination of actions taken by various ministries, departments and, Central and State law enforcement agencies. The creation of the NCORD was a consequence of realisation of the fact that while different agencies in the country were taking separate action with regard to the respective mandates on drug supply and demand reduction, there was, however, a need for an effective coordination mechanism to synergize the efforts of all such ministries/agencies. The Narcotics Control Bureau itself was a creation of law to carry out the coordination function. The NCORD mechanism created in 2016 provided an effective instrument to aid the coordination work of the Government. The NCORD structure envisages monthly meetings by the DG of the NCB with all the intelligence and enforcement agencies of the country dealing with drug matters for matters of operational coordination. In addition, quarterly meetings with the inclusion of the policy-making ministries and annual meetings at the level of Home Secretary are also envisaged.

This NCORD mechanism was reinforced in 2019. The Ministry of Home Affairs had taken a keen interest in analysing the functioning of the NCORD and on 29 July 2019, the NCORD mechanism was restructured to gear up for the existing challenges. The main focus of the restructuring was coordination in policy matters and improvement of the mechanisms for handling field-level issues. The restructuring of NCORD has taken care of the emerging situation which includes:

- Large increase in number of opioids users in the country
- Increased cross-border heroin trafficking including through maritime route
- Illicit cultivation of poppy and cannabis
- Diversion of opium from licit cultivation to illicit channels
- Threat of India emerging as a manufacturing centre for synthetic opioids such as Fentanyl
- Diversion of precursors and their trafficking to drug-producing neighbouring countries
- Trafficking and abuse of pharmaceutical preparations
- Multiplicity of stakeholders/agencies in the government

The restructuring of NCORD has created a four-tier structure with an apex committee at the centre level headed by Home Secretary, Executive Committee at the Central level headed by Special Secretary (IS), State-level committees headed by chief secretaries of the concerned states and district level committees headed by district SSPs/SPs/DCsP. The structure has provided a mechanism for proper coordination in which the vision of the apex committee gets percolated and implemented at the field formation level. It has also created an opportunity to understand field level issues and necessary solutions for the same can be effected.

National Action Plan for Drug Demand Reduction

The Ministry of Social Justice & Empowerment has been entrusted with the task of prevention and rehabilitation. The preventive strategies include education and awareness programmes and the rehabilitation programmes harbinger around the proper identification of addicts and providing them counselling, treatment and rehabilitation at personal, psychological and vocational fronts. The action plan has envisaged a holistic approach in which a person is an integral part of society and thus any rehabilitation and prevention has to be worked through society. The objectives of the plan are as follows:

- Awareness and education about ill effects of drug use
- Developing human resources
- Research and training
- Community-based services
- Undertaking demand reduction efforts
- Alleviating consequences of drug dependence

Data have shown that the dependence on opiates has emerged as the most significant problem. It is especially aggravated in the border areas of the Northwestern and Northeastern parts of India. It is clear, therefore, that the trafficking from across-the-border has been responsible for large amounts of opiates in the country causing severe addiction in these areas. This finding closely mirrors the concern expressed of the PM relating to cross-border trafficking of drugs.

Creation of Joint Consultative Committee

The MHA has taken another major decision by setting up a coordination mechanism to monitor major drug cases in India. The decision was taken after reviewing the large quantity of seizures of narcotics drugs which have taken place from 2017 onwards. The cases include seizure of heroin from the Gujarat coast and at Attari border. The investigation of these cases clearly points to the fact that there is a nexus of drug trafficking organisations based in Pakistan and Afghanistan. There are reasons to believe that these drug trafficking organisations have relations with the militants/terrorist organisations of these countries. In the light of these assessments, a Joint Consultative

Committee (JCC) was formed on 19 July 2019. The JCC, under the chairmanship of DG, Narcotics Control Bureau, has a role to play in all aspects of major drug cases including linkages with other organised crime syndicates, insurgency, terrorism and money laundering. The JCC has a supervisory role in the investigation of these cases for effective prosecution and to identify any networks emerging during investigation.

The JCC has held several meetings till now and has been successful in unearthing the inter connection between several large seizure cases of heroin that were effected by different agencies off the Gujarat coast. Cases taken up by the JCC are as under:

- 6 January, 2020: Seizure of 35 kg of heroin from a boat off the Gujarat (western) coast
- 20 May, 2019: Seizure of 218 kg of heroin from a boat off the Gujarat (western) coast
- March, 2019: Seizure of 100 kg of heroin from a boat in Gujarat
- 2017: Seizure of 1,445 kg of heroin from the cargo ship MV *Henry* in Gujarat

During deliberations of the JCC, it became apparent that these cases were the handiwork of the same criminal network that was operating from Pakistan and was involved in the following major seizure cases in Sri Lanka and Maldives:

- March, 2020: Seizure of 475 kg in Sri Lanka (Indian connections found and same under probe)
- February, 2020: Seizure of 294 kg in Sri Lanka
- November, 2019: Seizure of 224 kg in Sri Lanka
- October, 2019: Seizure of 70 kg in Maldives
- July/August, 2019: Seizure of 155 kg in Sri Lanka

The NDA Government tightened the screws on several most wanted underworld dons in India and abroad. Organised crime activities have drastically fallen in Mumbai, Delhi and Ahmedabad. Some gangs have been dismantled permanently. The seizure of Dawood's properties worth Rs. 15,000 crore, despite the best possible efforts of the Pakistan Government, in the UAE has given a blow to D-Company operations worldwide. Two close aides of Dawood—Chhota Shakeel and Tiger Memon—have been designated by the US Government as key drug traffickers for their roles as part of the D Company and sanctions have been slapped on them. Dawood was earlier named as a Specially Designated Global Terrorist in October 2003 when Atal Bihari Vajpayee was the PM of India. Trust and better understanding between the governments and security and intelligence agencies have led to close cooperation and stringent actions by foreign countries.

However, there are still some difficulties. In the Constitutional framework, police is a State subject. Most of the states face resource crunch to provide adequate resources to the different wings of the criminal justice system. Also, there is no central-level agency to coordinate the efforts of state police organisations and central agencies. There is no agency to collect, collate, analyse, document and function as a central pool for exchange of information about inter-state and international gangs. Problems of coordination do occur between the Centre and the State governments and between states due to differences in political perceptions. The nexus between criminals and politicians, politicians and bureaucrats, criminals and police, criminals and economic lobbyists, media persons and criminals or politicians do pose formidable challenges for the law enforcement agencies. The issue of dual criminality does help the members of organised crime syndicates if the criminals operate in more than two countries having variations in criminal laws, especially in drug trafficking cases.

The world communities and governments have to be doubly cautious regarding terrorist organisations joining hands with underworld gangs. Such matchmaking is a real threat and pose a considerable danger to international peace and security. When the world has one medical science, one engineering, one architecture, one humanity, why can't it have one set of stringent anti-terror and anti-organised crime laws?

5

Technology in Support of National Security

Alok Joshi

One of the common refrains encountered is how would the Indian state respond if there is an indication of a likely attack like what happened in Mumbai on 26 November 2008, also referred to as 26/11? Has anything changed to expect a more robust response from our security setup? What capacities have we built using technology as a prime mover? To appreciate what difference use of technology has made, it would be worthwhile to reimage how an episode like 26/11 would be handled in the present.

The initial input of likely movement of Lashkar terrorists by the sea route would trigger off a set of actions: the data bases would be checked for profiles of all known activists who have fallen off the radar, their communication devices would be identified and linked to trace their location as well as for content, a cyber operation would be launched to hack into the Lashkar-e-Taiba (LeT) control room for eavesdropping on internal communications, satellite imageries would be examined to keep a track on movements from and into the Lashkar camps and Light Detection and Ranging (LIDAR) images would be constructed to get a 3D look at the training camps. As the likely targets come to be known, facial recognition would be deployed to work on the inputs received from CCTV cameras in their proximity. Scanned images would be compared with databases and available profiles of Lashkar suspects picked up from hacked databases of that outfit. If the inputs continued to indicate any seaborne movement, collaboration with the Indian Navy and the Coast Guard would assist in the identification of non-white shipping in close proximity of the shore line apart from zoning in on the Thuraya communications in geo-fenced fields closer to the same. Closer home, drones would be deployed to assist ground forces. All this flow of information and data would be fused and worked upon to throw up red flags on the basis of algorithms worked out in consultation with the intelligence and security agencies. In the event of a shootout, autonomous weapons could be deployed if the need arose.

The above scenario is not a far-fetched one and the capabilities described have been painstakingly built over the past five to six years. Today, technology has been harnessed in a major way in the cause of safeguarding the nation.

The general elections in 2014 were held under the shadow of threats from Pakistan-based militant outfits including the LeT and the Jaish-e-Mohammad both in Jammu &Kashmir and in the mainland, a raging extremist movement was being witnessed in the states of Chhattisgarh, Jharkhand, Maharashtra and Odisha and undercurrents of unchallenged militancy in the Northeast of Myanmar-based insurgency groups. The response of the State to these challenges was influenced more by a conventional thought process that placed a premium on the functional role of individual security organisations as per their mandate. To put it simply, the effort was to make the effectiveness of the response dependent on the performance of individual organisations.

With the coming of the Modi-led NDA government, a paradigm shift in strategic thinking has taken place wherein emphasis has been laid on developing synergies at the cutting-edge level among the various intelligence and security organisations to deliver the maximum result. Technology has played a significant role in creating platforms and processes to deliver those synergies. The challenge was not only to upgrade technologies but also to ensure that they adapted to the need of the hour and delivered the results that could be operationalised. Technology was further leveraged not only to reconnect the various parts of the security establishment but also to create a feedback mechanism to ensure that the lessons learnt were incorporated to improve upon the processes put in place.

One of the radical changes brought about by the Modi Government was to take a holistic view of the functioning of the security architecture. Thus, an agency like the National Technical Research Organisation (NTRO) was drafted as a participant in the Director General of Police Conference for the first time in its existence of over a decade plus. Set up in 2004 as a facilitator for collection of technical intelligence for not only the strategic community but also for the intelligence and security agencies, the NTRO remained on the margins and could never integrate itself as a dynamic factor in the security process. The reasons for this were myriad. What is of relevance is that the Modi Government recognised its potential and not only gave it the status of an intelligence agency but also ensured that the organisation integrated itself was an active contributor to deliver on the challenges of national security. The organisation was given a free hand to restructure and revamp, and very quickly expanded its work-force with persons of proven skills at the cutting edge level. The financial powers of the chairman were suitably enhanced to assist in the procurement process. Similarly, the National Critical Information Infrastructure Protection Centre (NCIIPC) was set up in 2014 under the aegis of the NTRO by an Act of Parliament with the mandate to protect the information infrastructure of the critical sectors of the country. It has, however, remained largely on paper. Constrained in both human and financial resources, the NCIIPC has struggled to fulfil its mandated role. A review undertaken by the National Security Advisor (NSA) loosened the shackles and set the organisation on a growth trajectory.

One of the earliest tests of the new strategy of integration of technology capabilities with the needs of the strategic and intelligence community came at the time of the terror attacks on Pathankot in January 2016 and in September at Uri. The output received from various platforms of technical intelligence was one of the key factors in shaping our response. Whether it was tracking the movement of terrorist outfits and identification of key players or pinpointing the various training camps which by themselves always had the propensity to shift locations or the assessment of ground deployment of Pakistan forces on the basis of satellite imageries, all came through a highly integrated collection and dissemination system. Even after the Uri action, there was complete coordination between the Armed Forces and the technical intelligence apparatus. This was largely accomplished by embedding representatives of the consumer agencies within the NTRO and thereby ensuring not only a near real time flow of intelligence but swift recalibration of sensors leading to sharper focus in coverage as a result of constant feedback received from the latter. Another key change was to avoid unnecessary duplication of effort among various agencies while, at the same time, ensuring that the expertise available across the board had access to interpret the technical inputs as they came in. This working loop of 'inputs-assessment-operationalisation-feedback-recalibration' not only ensured greater cooperation among different organisations but also led to a better understanding of each other's capabilities and limitations. A broad inter-agency consensus followed as to which agency needed to be strengthened in which areas depending upon its core competencies and thus avoiding turf battles and frittering away of finite resources amongst too many claimants.

The Balakot strike in February 2019 once again established the importance of technology in meeting the demands of national security. Following the Pulwama attack on the CRPF convoy leading to a loss of 40 lives and with Uri already providing a template of a likely response from the political leadership, it was imperative that the same should be effective and timely. The convergence of intelligence from communication intercepts indicated the presence of terrorist camps of *Jaish* in Balakot. This was further reinforced by cyber operations directed on the target area and also satellite imagery. Further details worked out the presence of Pakistan air defence elements through electronic intelligence and collation of all available information and its analysis against historical data available gave a clear assessment to work upon. The rest, as they say, is history.

The application of technology in support of national security is not limited to acquisition of cutting edge technical assets but the manner in which they are deployed, their customisation for local conditions and, more importantly, the development of human resources to man the systems. It also entails the capability to indigenize the systems and build capacities for a 'Make in India' effort. Recognising this important element, the Government has drawn up a well-structured policy to encourage local industry and start-ups to engage in this growing field, particularly in areas that demand a high level of software engineering skills. Thus, an ecosystem has gradually developed in the field of high resolution imagery, drone applications, cyber security, communication technologies and autonomous weapons.

One of the areas that has seen commendable progress is in the field of data management, data exploitation and data security .With the emphasis on digitisation of the economy; it was felt early that there was a need to focus on Big Data Analytics in order to find solutions to security issues. Thus a Geographic Information System (GIS) were developed on which overlays of data could be structured to enable policy planners and those in the field to visualise the ground zero conditions and look for solutions accordingly. The fusion of data flows from telecommunications, cyber, satellite imageries and airborne sensors like drones and the resulting assimilation of the same gave an opportunity to gain insights that would have been otherwise difficult to discern. The interlinking of data of intelligence and security agencies is very much on the anvil and would revolutionise the way security issues are assessed and handled. The capacity to anticipate and pre-empt developing threats and mitigate them in near real time would be a leap forward in the area of national security.

The thrust towards digitisation and increasing demands on the cyber network has exposed the information infrastructure of the critical sectors to various vulnerabilities. Transport, financial, power, health and e-governance are some of the areas in the civilian domain that need extra protection. It is not too difficult to imagine the consequences of a successful attack on the financial sector if it results in the paralysis of the stock exchanges or banking transactions. Similar would be the impact of cyber attacks on the transport sector, particularly relating to air traffic management or goods/passenger movement over rail links. On several occasions, India has suffered heavy outages when the grids had failed, resulting in disruption of the distribution networks. The telecom sector is equally vulnerable to disruption as there is an increasing use of IP protocols for directing communication traffic. Recognising the sensitivity of the issue, the NCIIPC was encouraged to interact proactively with private enterprises to formulate a suitable strategy. This has resulted in setting up of cyber ranges and identification and nurturing of human resources with the intent to develop specialised skills in specific sectors. There has been much emphasis laid on voluntary disclosure of vulnerabilities and application of Artificial Intelligence for working out solutions for identifying and thwarting cyber attacks. This has gone a long way in strengthening the national security profile of the nation.

One of the areas where the use of technology has been encouraged is in relation to developing capabilities in the states. The NTRO took the lead in setting up of a cyber security and cyber forensic centre in Haryana followed by Assam, Uttarakhand and Punjab. This has not only strengthened Centre-State coordination but also led to development of common protocols and training by domain specialists of a large pool of police officers in the areas of cyber security and forensics. In Uttarakhand, a drone research centre has been set up for working out customised applications as also for handling and exploiting the imagery data collected. The Centre is also engaged in working on anti-drone technologies following the recent examples of drones being deployed for attacks on oil facilities in Saudi Arabia and on human targets in conflict zones. This is a new emerging threat to national and, particularly, VVIP security.

National security is an all-encompassing concept which goes beyond security of external borders or internal stability of the country. It encompasses not only threats to the sovereignty of the country but also efforts at destabilisation by accentuating ethnic, religious or ideological faultlines. This is all the more relevant considering that the concept of 'national power' has undergone a dramatic change and is no longer a function of the strength of the Armed Forces or the capacity of a nation to project its power outwards. The collapse of the Soviet Union and the rise of Communist China are examples of how power can be lost and gained without engaging in any widespread conflict. National security looks beyond power projections and is the sum of capabilities of a country to develop and mobilise its economic potential while at the same time reducing inequities within its system and building up capabilities to respond to hitherto unknown threats. While threat assessment in these times remains a dynamic concept—what was a threat earlier could transform itself into an opportunity—it is nevertheless important that a nation remains alert to the developing situations particularly in a wired world where globalisation and pan-national institutions play a lead role in firming up or even influencing policy choices. In this regard, technology can become our greatest asset.

The Government has recognised its potential and correspondingly put in place a national security architecture that is designed to take into account data on these rapid developments across the world from multiple channels, synthesise them and then analyze trends that would impact upon national security. The setting up of the office of the National Cyber Security Coordinator and three deputies to the NSA has given policy planners an edge in comprehending global trends along with a comprehensive view of how different nations are responding and to take a coherent view as to what would be the best response while formulating policy. The COVID-19 pandemic is a case in point. What other nations looked upon as a limited localised problem restricted to China was appreciated quickly as a major threat to the health and safety of our citizens. India's effective response included early evacuation of affected citizens from Wuhan, their quarantining at sanitized locations and subsequent handling of the crisis as per local conditions. Technology in the form of communication surveillance, deployment of drones for sanitization, cyber products in the form of apps to track and forewarn citizens in hot zones and analysis of data for gaining insights are all examples of how technology has been applied to cope and deal with the pandemic.

What does the future portend for the deployment of emerging

technologies in support of national security? Will the current pandemic crisis force a rethink as to how best to harness the software power of the nation in addressing emerging threats? Will a comprehensive approach take shape in conceptualisation of national security *per se*? It is apparent that a crisis, like COVID-19, can paralyze a nation and threaten its social fabric. Given the nature of such threats that can originate from distant lands, India will have to have appropriate response mechanisms in place. The answers would also lie in reading the global headwinds in a timely manner, analyzing them for their likely impact and then shaping policy actions. The impact of these policy manoeuvres would then have to be studied both in terms of their impact on people but also on the external environment. The importance of capturing data from different channels and the capacity to work on it cannot be overemphasised. The very task of building up data banks, linking them together and extracting meaningful conclusions from them would itself be a herculean task. It would involve building up sensors to capture the data, networks to carry it, capacities for Big Data Analysis, protecting the data through developing state-of-the-art encryption technologies and finally working out the platforms that could be used to execute policies and monitor the feedback and bring it back into the loop of decision making.

A relook at the recruitment and procurement process for building up both human resources and hardware capacities is called for and has already been discussed in the Government. There is a need for very robust public-private cooperation in these areas as a large pool of talents to address the above issues lies outside the government. Moreover, data collection by its very nature is intrusive and issues relating to data privacy need to be addressed without compromising on the demands of national security. Technology being largely a neutral factor could assist in building up protocols that could bring greater understanding with the general public and address their misgivings.

In the foreseeable future, technology will continue to play a pivotal role in shaping our national security perceptions and responses. This presupposes that capacities are in place to gather data from diverse sources and analyse them, to disseminate among a large number of stake holders and to create common platforms where they could be discussed among domain experts and to create networks both within and outside the government to enable such interactions. Acquisition of technology is not an end *per se* but a starting point of a series of processes that ultimately lead to qualitative changes in the appreciation and understanding of the national security environment. It entails changes in our traditional ways of functioning and calls for streamlining of processes, structural changes in decision making and out-of-the-box solutions to hitherto intractable issues including timely acquisition of technologies, flexibility in recruitment processes, predictable and fair engagement with private enterprises, avoidance of turf battles amongst security organisations, etc. The Government has been able to set up a security architecture that is seized of these issues and would be able to comprehensively address them and create an environment where technology is harnessed to the maximum in achieving national security objectives.

6

Forging Ahead: A New Strong India under Modi 2.0

Ranjit K. Pachnanda

Modi 2.0 envisions transformation of India into a New India. A country that is strong, secure, prosperous and invincible.... The inspirational vision and sterling leadership of the Prime Minister has brought about an overhaul in the security scenario in the country in all aspects—be it countering external threats or the threats of terrorism, naxal insurgency, border security or disaster security. The Government has deftly dealt with and handled all security challenges in the interest of the nation.

It has been a year since the formation of the Union Territories of J&K and Ladakh—a momentous achievement to rejuvenate and resurge Indian unity and development in J&K. Prior to that, terrorism had devastated the region leading to untold misery as about 41,500 people were killed in J&K from 1989 till August 2019. Invisible enemies fighting unholy proxy wars had attempted to threaten Indian democracy.

Post abrogation of Article 370, the Prime Minister rightly expects Kashmir to lead from the front as it now stands integrated with India in the true sense of the term. The people of J&K have the same rights, benefits and prospects as those in the rest of the country. Domicile certificate is now the basic eligibility condition for recruitment. The Indian Constitution is now applicable to J&K; consequently 170 Central laws have now become applicable in J&K, guaranteeing justice and fairness to the underprivileged. The repudiation of Articles 370 and 35A has heralded a new dawn of empowerment, equity and development. The rights of women marrying outside the UT now stand fully protected and gender discrimination has ended. The special status of Articles 370 and 35A had insulated the state from the rest of India leaving it backward as money was siphoned into vested pockets and did not reach the common man.

On November 7, 2015, the Prime Minister announced a Reconstruction Plan of Rs. 80,068 crore. Accordingly, Kashmir has witnessed a new sunrise by reinforcing governance, accelerating development, building infrastructure, generating employment, broadening social inclusion, providing humanitarian relief and promoting growth. Long years of unrest had adversely affected the state's democratic institutions, particularly those at the grassroots level. Immediately after the formation of the UT of J&K, panchayati raj institutions were established and made functional and Rs. 366 crore was released directly to 4,483 panchayats.

The Prime Minister has transformed the 'Tasveer' of J&K and the 'Taqdeer' of the people by more than fulfilling their aspirations. Nearly 506 of the 2,273 developmental projects stand completed while 963 projects are scheduled for completion by March 2021. Some of the major projects completed are IIT Jammu and Srinagar-Leh transmission line while works in mega projects including the Z Morh, Zoji La and New Banihal tunnels and some major roads are being executed on a war footing. Rs. 881 crore was earmarked for rebuilding health institutions and 60 of the 144 projects have been completed. There has been a major progress in hydro-power generation and flood management of the Jhelum River, Jhelum–Tawi Recovery Project, Chenab Bridge (the highest railway bridge in the world), connectivity of Kashmir by rail, mega-multi projects line Ujh and Shahpur Kandi as also the 330 MW Kishenganga project.

To promote transparency, the Modi Government has instituted a portal, namely, the J&K Infrastructure Monitoring System (JKIMS), by which the progress of work is physically monitored on real-time basis and the status of project implementation can be accessed by any individual. There has been a creation of 45,000 employment opportunities, vigorous road construction works, process of setting up of over 330 schools and colleges and a university, improved medical infrastructure including two AIIMSs, beginning of a light rail and public transport system, welfare measures for all including housing, implementation of women and child welfare schemes, support to farmers, orchardists and unorganised workers, expansion of tourism facilities, sports infrastructure and border area development.

To achieve 24x7 power for all, 60 per cent of works have been completed. J&K achieved 100 per cent household electrification which has rekindled the hope of many who had never seen electricity in their lives. Household water connections have reached 43 per cent of rural households which is double the national average of 21 per cent; a road map has been prepared to ensure 100 per cent coverage of piped water supply to all 18.16 lakh rural households by December 2021. Under the Pradhan Mantri Gram Sadak Yojana, J&K has embarked on constructing 5,300 km of road by 2020-21.

The Modi Government has rationalised reservation rules to benefit marginalised sections which have remained either unrepresented or under-represented. Kashmiri migrants have benefited from a serious of welfare measures like employment, transit accommodation and monthly financial assistance. Law and order has improved and violence has reduced. Terrorism and the misery of people are coming to an end, despite Pakistan's frustrated efforts to activate its "deep state" again to heat up the environment, even during the COVID pandemic. Abrogation of Article 370 has led to exasperation in the ranks of the terrorists; local recruitment of terrorists has dwindled. Pakistan is now encountering triple frustration—first, at the abrogation of Article 370; second, at the snub it has faced in all international fora where it has raised the Kashmir issue and, third, at the fact that all its efforts to initiate terrorist acts have only resulted in their constant decimation in encounters.

The formation of the Union Territory of J&K has not only witnessed development but also evoked patriotism and restored the confidence of the people in the Constitution of India and our robust democratic system of a united sovereign India with Justice, Liberty, Equality and Fraternity assuring the dignity of the Indian and unity and integrity of the nation. The pro-active measures being taken by a determined government, under PM Modi, are ushering in a new era of peace, tranquillity and development, which will soon blossom and finally deliver the long awaited smile on the face of the people.

While the world was battling COVID-19 and this was the time when we needed to cooperate to fight this global enemy, China chose to embark on a misadventure in the Galwan Valley, which was more than ably thwarted by our brave soldiers.

In his address, Prime Minister Modi stated that 20 of our jawans were martyred but not before they taught a lesson to those who had dared to raise eyes towards "Bharat Mata". The Prime Minister assured the nation that our forces would spare no effort to protect our nation as today we have the capability to prevent anyone eyeing even an inch of our territory. He said the infrastructure in the border areas had improved greatly leading to heightened patrolling and close monitoring of movements there. The Armed Forces had been given a free hand to take all necessary steps.

The Prime Minister's visit to Ladakh to motivate the valiant soldiers protect our motherland was truly the reflection of a great leader and statesman, and will go down in the annals of history. It not only sent a firm and powerful message but also exhibited a show of solidarity of a united Atmanirbhar Bharat—a Swabhiman Bharat, a Shashakta Bharat, a Sangthit Bharat and an Ek Atma Bharat. The Prime Minister also stated that India would respond firmly to any attempts to transgress the Line of Actual Control. At Leh, the Prime Minister sent a strong message to China that "the age of expansionism is over".

China has always had, in its DNA, a devious nibbling annexation habit and policy, due to which the areas of differences increased since the Congress meekly turned a blind eye to the nibbling away of our territories by the Chinese through continuous transgressions and border violations. Though we entered into as many as six bilateral agreements in 1988, 1993, 1996, 2005, 2012 and 2013, we did not address the dispute over the Line of Actual Control (LAC). When the Chinese intruded and pitched tents deep inside our territory in Depsang, in 2013, Prime Minister Manmohan Singh merely mentioned in Parliament about the Chinese having a different perception about the LAC. Protocols, talks and understanding between delegations meant nothing to China which kept violating the decisions taken. Confidence Building Measures were being misused by the Chinese to resort to psychological warfare and "salami slicing". This is because after 1962, non-violence was considered the policy of the then government. Our inglorious defeat in 1962 was an outcome of Jawaharlal Nehru's follies and misreading after China's invasion and occupation of Tibet in 1950. Nehru was even forewarned by Sardar Vallabhbhai Patel yet he wilfully allowed his belief to prevail. Post-1962, what became even more unforgiving was the lack of military capabilities and infrastructure along the vulnerable borders.

It was only after Narendra Modi became the Prime Minister that strengthening the infrastructure became a national priority. Today, there has been a great stride forward in infrastructure development at the Indo-China border on the Indian side which has become a great deterrent for China. Had the infrastructural development started in the Congress regimes, India would have been in a much more dominating position today. Since 2014, the Modi Government has created a strong road network spearheaded by the Border Roads Organisation and the CPWD despite the small window, during the year, for construction, due to the treacherous winter. The Border Area Development Programme has been allocated Rs. 784 crore in the fiscal year 2020-2021. The creation of infrastructure "would help integrate these areas with the hinterland, create a positive perception of care by the country and encourage the people to stay on in the border areas leading to safe and secure border" as per the MHA. Border infrastructure has developed through comprehensive Integrated Border Management Systems—be it border outposts, border fencing, mobile towers, use of technology at the border and lighting. On the Indo-Tibet border, not only has the spread of roads increased, but also other infrastructure including helipads, tunnels and bridges.

At the same time there has been increased patrolling—be it long range patrols, short range patrols or joint patrols of the Army and the ITBP. Indian soldiers have always held their ground in several face-offs which regularly take place. Our regular patrols also enable us to assess Chinese activities, identify features of tactical importance, dominate infiltration routes, corroborate inputs and assert our presence. Post 2014, our patrols have been actively engaging, confronting and preventing any incursions from the other side. We are consistently asserting our right and not allowing any construction activity in our territory within the LAC. In Doklam, we stalled the construction of a road by the Chinese which would have adversely affected our strategic interests. This was certainly a diplomatic victory for India. It is only after this that China became more wary of India's diplomatic and military might under Prime Minister Modi.

Work on a link road, part of an infrastructure project of a strategic road in Ladakh, is one of the factors which seemed to have pushed China into their misadventure on 15 June 2020 when they were given a bloody nose by our valiant soldiers. Another reason which could have irked China is the fact that India did not support the Belt and Road Initiative (BRI), which was not advisable from our security point of view. The BRI was a project by China to establish its dominance in global trade and this included the China-Pakistan Economic Corridor, which is not acceptable to India and it passes through Pakistan-occupied Kashmir. Other factors which could have added salt to China's wounds could have been the friendly relations between India and the USA and the formation of the two Union Territories of J&K and Ladakh and the abrogation of Article 370. This only reflects Chinese vulnerability and the Galwan aggression only reflects its desperate action.

Prime Minister Modi's policy towards China has been a judicious mix of diplomatic, military and economic strategies. Modi and President Xi Jinping have had as many as 18 summit meetings in the past six years, including two informal meetings at Mamallapuram and Wuhan. Several other meetings have been held at different levels. The 15th meeting of the WMCC (Working Mechanism for Consultation and Coordination) was held on 24 June 2020, in which India stressed on respecting the LAC and both sides agreed to expeditiously implement the 6 June understanding on disengagement and de-escalation. Having started the process of de-escalation, China again chooses to breach this understanding.

While diplomatic parleys should continue, it is imperative to continue strengthening both our infrastructural and military build-up to muzzle and choke the dragon in case it attempts to spit fire again. On the international front, our policy has always been that a peaceful, stable and secure region demands a climate of trust, cooperation, non-aggression, respect for international rules and norms, sensitivity to each other's interests and a peaceful resolution of differences. There is a need for institutional capacity to deal with traditional and non-traditional threats, especially terrorism, drug trafficking and transnational crime. India is committed to the evolution of a global architecture which would be open, transparent, inclusive, rule based and anchored in international law. However, though India is a peaceful nation, it shall negotiate only from a position of strength. And this can happen only under the strong leadership of Prime Minister Modi. Regarding internal security, apart from J&K, the principal focus has remained on improving the security scenario in the Northeastern States, combating Left Wing Extremism and maintaining peace in the hinterland of the country. The Government since 2014 has contained cross border infiltration, promoted economic activity, provided relief to victims and strengthened the state's security apparatus.

In the Northeast region, the Government followed a multipronged strategy to effectively deal with insurgent and militant activities. The approach includes security measures, civic action programmes, development works, negotiations with groups which abjure violence and seek resolution of their demands within the framework of the Indian Constitution to come into the mainstream of national life. As a result, a number of outfits have come forward for talks with the

Government and have entered into Suspension of Operations agreements and some of them have signed Memorandum of Settlements and dissolved themselves. The Government has devised programmes for capacity building of State forces in intelligence collection, responding to terror incidents and investigation of terror cases. The number of insurgency incidents and security force personnel killings has drastically declined since 1997. Coordinated counter-insurgency operations have led to neutralisation and arrest of several militants and recovery of a large number of weapons, ammunition and explosives and a drastic reduction of kidnapping/abduction cases.

While there is almost no insurgency in Tripura and Mizoram, there has been a marked improvement in the security situation in other States of the region. In 2018, insurgency related violence declined by 48 per cent in Meghalaya, 40 per cent in Arunachal Pradesh, 16 per cent in Assam and 24 per cent in Manipur compared to 2017.

The Modi Government has countered Left Wing Extremist (LWE) insurgency, adopting an integrated and positive approach by addressing the areas of security, development and promoting good governance simultaneously. To achieve this, a National Policy and Action Plan has been put in place that adopts a multi-pronged strategy in the areas of security, development, and ensuring rights and entitlements of local communities. Other security-related measures include providing Central Armed Police Forces (CAPFs), sanction of India Reserve (IR) battalions, modernisation and upgradation of the state police under the Umbrella Scheme 'Modernisation of Police Forces' (MPF scheme), re-imbursement of security-related expenditure under the Security Related Expenditure (SRE) Scheme, strengthening of Special Intelligence Branches/Special Forces of the states and fortification of police stations under the Special Infrastructure Schemes (SIS), providing helicopters for anti-LWE operations, assistance in training of the state police, sharing of intelligence, facilitating inter-state coordination, Community Policing and Civic Action programmes. Simultaneously, the basic infrastructure like roads and telecom connectivity were improved. The capacity of state governments has been enhanced to tackle the LWE menace in a concerted manner.

In the last few years there has been a significant decline in LWE violence as well as the geographical spread of LWE. At the same time, the development outreach by the Centre has seen an increasingly large number of LWE cadres shunning the path of violence and returning to the mainstream. The Government remained committed to curbing the funding of terrorism and anti-national activities.

Even though border management remains the most complex operation due to a large magnitude of concerns, the effective management of borders is vital to national security. India has 15,106.7 kilometres of land border and a coast line of 7,516.6 km. India has a border of 4,096.8 km with Bangladesh, which is guarded by the BSF. With Pakistan, also guarded by the BSF, it has a border of 3,323 km. A border of 3,488 km with China, which is guarded by the ITBP and a border of 1,751 km with Nepal, guarded by the SSB, which also guards the 699-km border with Bhutan. The Assam Rifles dominates the 1643 km border with Myanmar. India also shares 106 km with Afghanistan in POK. Besides, the Indian Army is guarding the land border along the LOC on the Pakistan Border and the LAC on the China border.

As mentioned earlier, the government has laid stress on construction of the border fencing, flood lighting, Border outposts, building roads, development of Integrated Check-posts as also developmental works along the Indo Pakistan, Indo Bangladesh, Indo China and Indo Nepal Borders. Coastal security has also been enhanced. The Government has also started a Comprehensive Integrated Border Management System (CIBMS), where physical fencing does not exist along the Indo-Bangladesh border; this includes integration of manpower, sensors, networks, intelligence and Command and Control Solutions. The pilot project has also been undertaken along the Indo-Pakistan border. The government is implementing the Border Area Development Programme through State governments as part of a comprehensive approach to border management with the view to meet special development needs and the well-being of people living in remote and inaccessible areas near the international border.

Despite concerns regarding the Indian border relating to security, infrastructure, economy and perception management, apart from issues of illegal migration, drug-arms-human trafficking, smuggling, induction of Fake Indian Currency Notes and activities of Indian insurgent groups, our valiant border forces guarding our borders and enforcement agencies have, very ably, dominated the borders in all aspects. Simultaneously, there has also been coordinated action on all fronts regarding fake currency and money laundering and controlling caste, communal and sectarian violence.

Concerted action has always promptly been taken to counter any onslaught against national security, without adopting a policy of shifting convenience. The tirade against the threat to national security has been painstaking and efforts to counter it have been more than dedicated and relentless. And this has only been possible because of the resolute leadership of the highest order. The Modi Government believes in keeping every citizen, who is an equal stakeholder in national security, secure from all kinds of threats, both external and internal. Here lies the accomplishment of a determined government under the leadership of Prime Minister Modi, which wants India to be one and committed to the welfare of all its citizens. Here lies the accomplishment of a determined government under Prime Minister Modi, which wants India to be one and committed with the greatest of welfare for the benefit of all its citizens.

7

The Return of India's Stolen Heritage

Sujan R. Chinoy

Media reports in mid-September 2020 reported that the United Kingdom had returned to India stolen idols of Lord Ram, Sita and Lakshman dating back to the 15th century. The idols had been stolen from a temple in Tamil Nadu in 1978. Earlier, the British Government had returned to India the Brahma-Brahmani sculpture which was stolen from the World Heritage site *Rani Ki Vav,* a 12th century bronze Buddha and other antiquities dating back to the 17th century and a Shiva statue that belonged to the Ghateshwar Temple in Baroli in Rajasthan. These returned antiquities can be deemed to be a symbolic reward for the people of India coinciding with the 70th birthday celebrations of Prime Minister Narendra Modi.

On 14 July 2017, *The Print* ran a story titled "Under PM Modi, India got back more stolen antiquities in 3 years than the UPA government in 10 years". It said that since 2014, the Modi Government had succeeded in bringing back to India 24 antiquities that had either been stolen or smuggled abroad. In contrast, it quoted the Archaeological Survey of India (ASI) as stating that during 2009-2014, the Government had only managed to retrieve one item. The then

Director (Antiquities) of the ASI was quoted as saying that there had been a definite spurt in retrieving India's lost antiquities during the Modi years, whereas between 2004-2009 no such objects were brought back, and between 1976 and 2013, only a total of 13 antiquities had been brought back to India.

During a visit to London, one can chance upon the London Museum and there come face to face with the famous Parthenon Marbles, more popularly known as the Elgin Marbles. These, like so many other antiquities, had been removed from the Temple of Parthenon in Greece between 1801 and 1812 by agents of Thomas Bruce, the 7th Earl of Elgin, and shipped back to Britain. Elgin had subsequently made specious claims of having obtained a "firman" from the Ottoman Empire which ruled Greece during that period, but this has always been disputed. Under strong social opprobrium, including criticism from Lord Byron who described Elgin's acts as akin to vandalism and looting, the latter handed over the collection to the British Government in 1816 since when they have formed part of the display of Greek antiquities in the London Museum. The remaining collection is housed in the Acropolis Museum in Greece, facing the Temple of Parthenon, with space vacant for display of the stolen collection as and when Britain takes the moral call of the conscience.

Greece and Egypt, like India and China, boast two of the ancient world's richest civilisations. Their antiquities were largely discovered during the 18th to early 20th century, a period that coincided with the Industrial Age in Europe and the formal and informal depredations of antiquities from the ancient world carried out by colonial powers or self-proclaimed explorers and archaeologists who were little more than well-heeled collectors who could afford to finance missions of discovery in vulnerable parts of the world.

Apart from the Elgin Marbles, one has heard of the Nefertiti Bust, part of some 5,000 antiquities spread around museums and private collections around the world that Egypt has sought the return of. Today, the bust of Queen Nefertiti, 3,400 years old, discovered by German archaeologist Ludwig Borchardt in 1912 and taken to Germany the following year, is part of the famous Egyptian collection at the Neues Museum in Berlin. Germany has yet to return it to Egypt.

Turkey has for years tried to secure the return of its antiquities from some of the world's largest museums including the Met, the Louvre, and the Pergamon. It has especially mounted a strong campaign to bring back the more than 2000-year-old marble torso called "Old Fisherman from Aphrodisias," which is currently on display in the Pergamon Museum in Berlin, but the German authorities have so far refused to return it, claiming that the piece was brought there in 1904 as part of an old collection of antiquities, apparently bought from an "art market" and therefore "legal".

In recent years, China has also made a concerted effort to bring home its antiquities, often with the central government assisted by generous patriotic entrepreneurs who take pride in financing the purchase from international auctions for a reverse collection for display in the country's national museums. The UK, in particular, has been asked for the return of thousands of artefacts taken out of China over the centuries, including in times of strife such as the destruction of the Old Summer Palace in Beijing in 1860 and during the reprisals associated with the Boxer Rebellion in the late 19th century.

According to an article titled 'Antiquities Theft And Illicit Antiquities Trade in India', published on 22 October 2018 by Samayita Banerjee and co-author Ishani Ghorai[1], "In India between 1977 and 1979, nearly 3,000 thefts of antiquities were reported. In that same decade, more than 50,000 art objects were smuggled out of India as estimated by UNESCO. The growing demand in the antiquities market for Indian art objects has led to major destruction and vandalism of archaeological sites in the country. However, looking at this issue of 'theft' from simply a statistical perspective remains a problem in the case of post-Independence India".

The authors have cited the mystery novel written in 1974 by distinguished film-maker Satyajit Ray, as a part of his detective novel and short story series on the adventures of private detective Pradosh Chandra Mitter, popularly known as Feluda. This novel *'Kailash-e*

Kelenkari' was about the hunt for an illegally stolen yakshi head from the Kailash Temple at Ellora, India. The story, according to Samayita and Ishani, revolved around the search for the stolen head and the subsequent exposure of an intricate network in illegal antiquities trade. As they have rightly pointed out, "the story is popular for the mystery and the thrill that a good detective novel contains, but in composing it Ray highlighted one of the major problems that concerns the fate of historical sites of this country".

India, in the 19th century, was completely under the domination of the British. Officers of the Raj devoted a fair bit of their time to collecting the antiquities of India, shipping home to the British Isles many artefacts for private enjoyment of their association with the Empire and enrichment in retirement. They decided arbitrarily what was valuable and what could be bought, sold and exported out of the country. The Archaeological Survey of India was established in 1861, but, as Samayita and Ishani point out, it was particularly Lord Curzon (1898-1905) who took the initiative to oppose the removal of Indian artefacts to British museums and advocated their restoration of their place of origin. This was opposed by others who saw it as an infringement of the "rights of the British museums". Sadly, Indian antiquities continued to be removed from the country.

There are a number of laws in India to govern the entire spectrum of issues relating to archaeological finds and preservation and protection of antiquities and art treasures. But these have either proved insufficient or have been exploited due to a number of factors including lax vigil, organised crime that tasks the illegal theft and export of treasures, often with some abetment of corrupt middlemen and, occasionally, some officials.

The 1878 Treasure Trove Act requires the finder to report finding any object/objects to proper government agents. The Government can acquire it by recompensing the owner the market value of the object plus an extra 20 per cent. This was followed in pre-independent India by the 1904 Ancient Monuments Preservation Act that sought to protect monuments and sites of archaeological and historical significance. After Independence, the 1947 Ancient Monuments Preservation Act was followed by the 1958 Act which complemented the pre-Independence 1947 Antiquities Export Control Act which was intended to regulate the trade in antiquities and permit the licensed export of antiquities.

Demand for Indian art and antiquities surged in the second half of the 20th century. The decades of the 1950s and 1960s witnessed the smuggling of many Indian treasures, with art dealers in India and around the world taking advantage of lax vigil about certification of provenance. Art galleries and museums around the world began to acquire Indian antiquities, especially in the USA.

The 1972 Antiquities and Art Treasure Act, implemented in 1976, strictly banned the export of any sort of archaeological object and also imposed stricter vigilance on individual ownerships of such objects. In short, all archaeological objects and sites were taken under state possession and authority. Under this rule, attempts started to be made to get back stolen antiquities (Biswas 1991).[2]

As Samayita and Ishani point out, one of the most famous cases was that of the Pathur Nataraja. This bronze statue of Nataraja, belonging to the Chola period, found itself at the centre of a High Court case between 1984 and 1988. It was supposedly unearthed in 1976 by a landless labourer, Ramamoorthi, who sold it for money instead of informing the Collector of the region. The statue had passed through a series of buyers until it was bought by the Bumper Development Oil Company of Canada and subsequently sent to London for repairs, where it was identified as the stolen idol. The Nataraja was, however, won back by the Indian Government in 1988.[3]

Another example can be given of the Sivapuram Nataraja, which was stolen from a hoard of bronze idols in 1957. It fell in the hands of the American collector, Norton Simon, in 1973, who confessed that it was stolen. In his own words, as told to a *Times* of London reporter, 'Hell yes, it was smuggled, I spent between $15 million and $16 million over the last year on Asian Art, and most of it was smuggled.' He argued, in his defence, however, that it was not stolen (Davis 1997).[4] The idols were returned to India in 1986 after a ten-year lease to Simon.

These are, of course, a few of several major cases that can be mentioned in this article. Lord Curzon in his famous lecture delivered at the Asiatic Society on December 20, 1900, gave a list of acts of vandalism that had been carried out in the Bentinck era. These included the destruction of the Taj marbles, leasing of the gardens at Sikandra to executive engineers for the purpose of 'speculative cultivation', and, of course, during the time of the Mutiny, countless monuments were destroyed and looted. And although these acts of vandalism may not be as extreme as they were in the 19th century, they continue to persist.

Smuggling of antiquities was first detected in 1936 when a French national from Pondicherry was caught sending objects to France with the help of two local men. From Khajuraho alone over 100 erotic sculptures had been stolen from the period between 1965 and 1970. Among two very famous cases, one was the burglary at the Jaipur Palace Museum from where almost 1,750 miniature paintings were removed, and the other is the 1968 theft at the National Museum (New Delhi) where 125 pieces of antique jewellery and 32 rare gold coins went missing (Pal 1992).[5] Although post-Independence India seems notorious when it comes to illegal theft and trafficking in antiquities, pre-Independence India too witnessed much of the same. Apart from the vandalism that took place in the 19th century that has been mentioned above, there are instances from the following century as well. Perhaps the biggest example is the presence of several Indus Valley objects in the London Museum. But there will remain a difference in the magnitude of thefts since the terms 'foreign' and 'theft' had very different meanings in pre- and post-Independence India.

The most egregious case of the looting and sale of Indian antiquities in recent decades involves Subhash Kapoor, a New York-based art dealer who is accused of running a racket involving theft and smuggling of treasures from India for sale to art galleries and museums around the world through his Art of the Past gallery in Manhattan. He was arrested in 2011 from Frankfurt International Airport and extradited to stand trial in India where he is currently in jail in Tamil Nadu.

In 2008, an 11th century Chola period bronze statue of a Dancing Shiva (the Sripuranthan Nataraja idol) was stolen by a gang of thieves and local dealers, under specific tasking, from the defunct ancient Brihadeeshwarar temple, smuggled to the USA with false papers of provenance and then sold to the National Gallery of Australia for a whopping sum of US$ 5.1 million.

Of course, over the years, a number of individuals and entities have contributed to increased awareness and effort in tracking down such art. S. Vijay Kumar, co-founder of the India Pride Project, who works for a shipping company in Singapore, was instrumental in tracking down a number of stolen Indian antiquities in museums and galleries around the world, including in Australia.

The biggest change in recent years is the personal interest taken by Prime Minister Narendra Modi in the return of stolen and illegally exported Indian art and antiquities. On 5 September 2014, the then Prime Minister of Australia, Tony Abott, returned to Prime Minister Narendra Modi the Sripuranthan Nataraja idol as well as another piece, a sculpture of Ardhanariswara, which fuses Shiva and Parvati in a half-man-half-woman form, which was also sourced from Subhash Kapoor for more than USD 300,000 by the Art Gallery of New South Wales.

In his remarks at the joint press briefing, PM Modi expressed his gratitude thus, "*At first, I would like to convey to Prime Minister Abbott the deep sense of gratitude of 1.25 billion people of India for the efforts he has made to bring with him two ancient statues that were stolen from India. The moment we had conveyed our request for the return of these statues, his government took this decision with great speed. Prime Minister Abbott and the people of Australia have shown enormous respect and regard not only for our ancient treasure, but also for our cultural heritage*".

After Prime Minister Modi's Government took office in 2014, the authorities stepped up efforts to crack down on gangs involved in the theft and smuggling abroad of Indian idols. Working in tandem with the state authorities, particularly in Tamil Nadu, they disrupted a large network operating from Chennai to Mumbai with links to museums and art galleries around the world. Art dealer Deena Dayalan of Chennai was one of the leading suppliers of art to be investigated for his activities.

On 7 June 2016, at a ceremony attended by Prime Minister Modi, the USA committed to return to India 200 artefacts estimated to value more than US$ 100 million in the international market. These included statues, bronze and terracotta pieces, some dating back 2,000 years, which were stolen from places of worship across India. Speaking at a media briefing on the occasion of the Prime Minister's visit, the Ambassador of India to the USA, Arun Kumar Singh, said, "Now, in terms of the ceremony for return of a number of cultural artefacts, that was again very significant. It is an effort that has been ongoing for some time. There are a large number of cultural artefacts from India that have been illegally taken to different parts of the world. There is a certain number also in the USA. Governments in different countries including the USA have been working very actively with us to identify them and find a way to repatriate them to India. It's an ongoing process because some time processes have to be completed here in USA before the repatriation can be carried out, their legal judicial process and others, but for this particular ceremony, 12 pieces were identified as being ready to be handed back to the government and people of India. These are significant because some of them date back to a thousand years, from the period of the Chola Dynasty. Some of them date back to more than two thousand years, some terracotta pieces and others. So some very significant items have been handed over to us and of course now they will be repatriated to India".

Among them was a statue of Saint Manikkavichavakar, a Hindu mystic and poet from the Chola period (circa AD 850 to AD 1250) stolen from the Sivan temple in Chennai, and a bronze sculpture of Lord Ganesh estimated to be 1,000 years old.

The then official spokesman of the Ministry of External Affairs was asked at the media briefing as to what exactly had the Prime Minister said at the handing over ceremony regarding the return of India's stolen heritage. This is what he had to say in response to a question from Lalit Jha, correspondent of the PTI,

> *"Yes he did speak. Just look at my twitter handle and you will see some of the comments that Prime Minister made. Basically he talked about how these artefacts are not only India's link to its ancient civilisation but these are treasures which should be enjoyed by the entire world and yet there are*

> *people who engage in illicit trafficking of these treasures and in that context he really thanked the Obama Administration, President Obama in particular, the Attorney General. Her entire team, which has worked tirelessly for many years to build a water-tight case after which only the decision was taken to return these artefacts and in fact the Attorney General mentioned that this is the launch of a process to return as many as 200 artefacts to India. Today, 12 have been returned but the process is underway to recover all the lost, stolen artefacts from India. She did mention the name of a particular art dealer also who was engaged in this particular exercise and how, thanks to very strong cooperation between the US and Indian enforcement agencies, these artefacts are being brought back to India. Prime Minister delved at great detail on how his own state of Gujarat in fact is a repository of so many ancient treasures including the city of Dholavira, which dates back to the Mohenjo-Daro-Harappa period, 5,000 years of history, culture and how they connect between the past and the present. I think he really spoke with a lot of feeling, with a lot of emotion because of his own personal attachment to this project of returning India's cultural heritage".*

Speaking at the handing over ceremony, US Attorney General Loretta E. Lynch said that the artefacts were testimony to India's astounding history and beautiful culture and would be beginning their journey home. "It is my hope—and the hope of the American people—that this repatriation will serve as a sign of our great respect for India's culture; our deep admiration for its people; and our sincere appreciation for the ties between our nations".

Secretary of Homeland Security Jeh Johnson said in a statement, *"Protecting the cultural heritage of our global community is important work and we are committed to identifying and returning these priceless items to their countries of origin and rightful owners"*. He added that "it is the responsibility of law enforcement worldwide to ensure criminal smuggling organisations do not profit from the theft of these culturally and historically valuable items".

The majority of the antiquities repatriated in the ceremony were seizures made during Operation Hidden Idol, an investigation that was launched in 2007 after the Homeland Security Investigations (HIS) special agents in the USA received a tipoff about illegal shipments being made to the USA disguised as "marble garden table sets" imported by Subhash Kapoor, owner of Art of the Past Gallery, who awaits trial in India.

In September 2018, two antique statues worth hundreds of thousands of dollars in the international market, stolen from India and displayed at two American museums, were handed over to the Consul General of India in New York by the Manhattan District Attorney, Cyrus Vance Jr. These were 'Lingodhbhavamurti', a 12th century (Chola dynasty) granite sculpture depicting Lord Shiva from the Birmingham Museum in Alabama, and Manjusri, a phyllite Bodhisattva sculpture of the same vintage.

Growing up in a small town called Vadnagar in Mehsana district in Gujarat, the young Narendra Modi was steeped in Indian history and culture from a very tender age. At school, he had earned the moniker "audacious explorer". He grew up near the 4,500-year-old Sharmishtha Lake which was a work of earth and stone built to hold water, dating back to the Solanki period. It is still in use, with its ancient dam earthwork which is a mound of earth or stone built to hold water as an interesting example of the water retaining systems of the Solanki period. It is fed by the waters of the Kapila river which flows from the catchment area around the Aravalli hills. As a fourteen-year-old boy at school at Vadnagar, he acted in a school drama, playing the role of 19th century chieftain, Jogidas Khuman, who was a righteous man who lived the life of an outlaw fighting for his rights after his family was dispossessed of its lands.

Vadnagar is not a place one would normally associate with ancient history, but it occupies an important place in the history of early contacts between India and China. Visiting Vadnagar in 2017 for the first time after his electoral victory, Narendra Modi narrated to a public gathering that the President of China, Xi Jinping, had told him during his visit to Gujarat in September 2014 that Vadnagar, PM Modi's birthplace, had a special connection with Xian, the birthplace of the Chinese President. "*Chinese traveller Hiuen Tsang (also spelt as Xuan Zhuang) stayed at Vadnagar during his India visit and when he returned to China, he stayed in Xian, the hometown of Jinping,*" Narendra Modi had said to thundering applause from the crowd.

The ASI has carried out extensive excavations at Vadnagar in several phases, beginning in 1953-54 under noted archaeologist S.R. Rao. After a relatively long lull of about 50 years, the second phase of excavation was carried out by Y.S. Rawat of the State Archaeology Department of the Government of Gujarat at Vadnagar from 2006 to 2010 during Narendra Modi's tenure as Chief Minister. The third phase began in 2014-15 after Narendra Modi became the Prime Minister of India.

The excavations till date have revealed the presence of Buddhist monasteries. In his travelogue, Si-Yu-Ki (also spelt Xi You Ji, translated by British scholar, Samuel Beal, in 1884 and published as "The Buddhist Records of the Western World") dating back to the 7th century AD, Hieun Tsang has said that he saw 10 big Buddhist monasteries at Vadnagar during his stay in the ancient city. Narendra Modi told his audience that President Xi Jinping had not only taken him to his hometown, Xian, from where Hiuen Tsang launched his travels to India and where he finally returned, but that he had personally read out to him from Hieun Tsang's manuscripts about Vadnagar.

Hiuen Tsang has pronounced Vadnagar as 'O-nan-to-pu-lo', which translates into Anandapura, the name for the ancient city. In Hiuen Tsang's words, *"There are some ten sangharama with less than 1,000 monks. They follow the Hinayana sect of Buddhism and study in accordance with the Sammatiya school. There are several big Deva temples, and sectaries of different kinds visit them."*

Even as a boy, and later as a young man, Narendra Modi carried with him a deep sense of pride in India's ancient past. As he moved from Vadnagar on to a much bigger landscape at the state, national and then global level, his pride in India's ancient heritage was much in evidence as he put his own imprint onto the history of India. His was never the elitist approach to India's ancient past, nor any great scholarly examination of timelines and events. He has always had a sincere, heartfelt, earthy and realistic sense of being an inheritor, like the 1.25 billion people of India, of a legacy of a rich and timeless civilisation that predates by many centuries all that is today admired in the Western world. His passion for India's past and lessons from

India's own history and experience was first stirred up when he was living in a hard, yet ancient place like Vadnagar. This, no doubt, played a role in the kind of personal interest he took, and continues to take, in the return of India's heritage from around the world to its rightful owners—the people of India.

NOTES

1. Samayita Banerjee and Ishani Ghorai, "Antiquities Theft and Illicit Antiquities Trade in India", Sahapedia, October 22, 2018 at https://www.sahapedia.org/antiquities-theft-and-illicitantiquities-trade-india#_edn5
2. Biswas, S.S. (1991), Protecting the Cultural Heritage, New Delhi: Aryan Books International.
3. Samayita Banerjee and Ishani Ghorai, "Antiquities Theft and Illicit Antiquities Trade in India", Sahapedia, October 22, 2018 at https://www.sahapedia.org/antiquities-theft-and-illicitantiquities-trade-india#_edn5
4. Davis, R.H. (1997), Lives of Indian Images, Princeton: Princeton University Press.
5. Pal, H.B. (1992), The Plunder of Art, New Delhi: Abhinav Publications.

8

Securing India's Maritime Interests and Harnessing the Blue Economy

R.K. Dhowan

India is essentially a maritime nation with a glorious maritime heritage, and the Indian seaboard has been the vortex of intense maritime activity over centuries. The Indus Valley Civilisation which existed in the western part of the country dates back to 3300 BC and even today we have a dry dock at Lothal in Gujarat which dates back to 2200 BC. It is from these small ports that ancient seafarers sailed off to distant lands in Mesopotamia, ancient Egypt and the East coast of Africa. Kautilya's *Arthashastra* mentions the 'Nav Parishad' during the Mauryan Empire which is akin to the Admiralty Board for monitoring maritime issues.

On the East Coast of India and the southern part of the country, we had the seafaring kingdoms of the Kalingas, Cholas, Pandyas, Pallawas and the Cheras who sailed to distant countries in South East Asia and even today we can see glimpses of India's cultural heritage in these countries. India's maritime capabilities also made it an economically powerful country. As documented by the historian, Angus Madison, India had the largest GDP in the world till around AD 1500, with China being its closest competitor with India accounting for nearly 25 per cent of the world's wealth.

The British period in India was also one of extensive shipbuilding activity. Commencing in 1735, and over the next hundred years, Bombay Dockyard built about 144 merchant ships and 115 war vessels, including 84 gunships for the Royal Navy. The oldest warship afloat in the world today, HMS *Trincomalee,* which is now berthed in Hartlepool in the UK, was built in India. The national anthem of the United States of America was written by Francis Key in Baltimore onboard the ship HMS *Minden* which was built at Bombay Dockyard. The Treaty of Nanking ceding Hong Kong to the British was signed on 29 August 1842, onboard another famous warship HMS *Cornwallis,* which was also built in India.

Regrettably, when the transition took place from 'sail to steam' and 'wood to steel', India was left behind as we were then not part of the Industrial Revolution. The revival of our maritime capabilities took place only post-independence in the latter part of the 20th century, when our leaders realised that to be secure on land we needed to be supreme at sea.

Today, India occupies a dominant position in the Indian Ocean, as the country sits astride busy sea lines of communication, which transit across the Indian Ocean, over which nearly 120,000 ships transit every year carrying 66 per cent of the world's oil, 50 per cent of the world's container traffic and 33 per cent of the world's cargo traffic.

Our blue planet, the Earth, has a dominance of the maritime domain with over 70 per cent of the Earth's surface covered by water, nearly 80 per cent of the world population living within 200 nautical miles of the coast and about 90 per cent of the world's trade transiting by sea. Oceans are therefore central to life on Earth. They are rich in oil and mineral resources, they are suppliers of oxygen, absorbers of carbon-dioxide, a virtual heat sink, rich in bio-diversity and have emerged as the global economic highways for transit of trade. With the depletion of resources on land, humankind has turned towards the seas for resources and there is a misperception that oceans have an unending resource base and are an infinite sink, but nothing could be further away from reality. Over the past few decades, we are witnessing pollution of the seas and contamination of the natural marine habitat, resulting in an adverse impact of climate change on the oceans. Studies have indicated that almost 80 per cent of the pollutants in the seas emanate from land and if the current rate of pollution continues, in a few decades we will have more plastic in the oceans than fish.

The concept of a 'Blue Economy' has emerged as the new paradigm and harnessing the same could be interpreted as economic development of our maritime interests by efficient utilisation of marine resources with minimum impact on the environment and ensuring sustainable development of the oceans.

India has a unique maritime disposition with a natural outflow towards the seas with our island territories of the Andaman and Nicobar Islands in the Bay of Bengal and Lakshadweep Islands in the Arabian Sea. India has a coastline of 7,516 km and an Exclusive Economic Zone of over 2 million square kilometres. Approximately, 95 per cent of India's trade by volume and 77 per cent by value, transits by sea and foreign trade accounts for over 30 per cent of India's GDP.

India has vast maritime interests, which have a vital relationship with the nation's economic growth. In recent years, under the leadership of Prime Minister Shri Narendra Modi, there has been series of much needed initiatives and intense activity for sustainable development in the maritime domain, coupled with the transition from 'Look East' to the 'Act East' policy. These initiatives will act as catalysts to strengthen the growth of India as a credible maritime power. India's vast maritime interests are also enablers of our Blue Economy, and the entire span of maritime sectors is likely to witness significant growth in the coming years, and will also serve as avenues for maritime cooperation with other neighbouring countries.

India has 12 major ports and 200 non-major ports. The handling capacity of these ports which currently stands at approximately 1,500 million metric tons per annum is likely to increase to 2,500 million metric tons per annum over the next ten years. The Government of India has launched the ambitious Sagarmala project, which is a port-led development initiative based on four pillars of port modernisation, connectivity, port-led industrialisation and coastal community development. Sagarmala actually comprises about 150 integrated projects with a planned investment of about 60 billion US dollars. Development of green field port infrastructure could be an area of maritime cooperation which will also generate substantial employment in the maritime sector. The Sagarmala project would also enhance the connectivity of ports with the hinterland by multimodal road and rail connectivity and development of inland waterways.

India currently has approximately 14,500 km of navigable inland waterways and in the first phase, the Government is developing 6,000 km as five major national waterways. Currently, 94 per cent of freight in India moves by road or rail and development of inland waterways will enhance transportation over water, which is cheaper (economical), faster and cleaner. The planned development of additional inland waterways presents a huge opportunity for investment and growth in India.

The mercantile marine and shipping industry is also envisaged to grow in the near future. India currently has a merchant ship fleet of approximately 1,430 ships flying the Indian flag. While over 90 per cent of India's trade by volume transits by sea, the share of Indian shipping in India's foreign external trade has declined from about 30 per cent in the 1980s to approximately 7 per cent today. To enable India's growing foreign trade to be carried on Indian hulls, the Indian Government is providing incentives for Indian registered shipping and has initiated measures to increase the tonnage of 'Indian Controlled Shipping'. This will assist in correcting the imbalance between Flag and Trade.

India has a vibrant shipbuilding and warship building industry with 27 shipyards. Recently, the Government of India has given a major boost to the shipbuilding industry by according it special infrastructure status and permitting 100 per cent Foreign Direct Investment (FDI) in shipbuilding. Joint-venture partnerships between shipyards could be avenues for future maritime cooperation, and enhancing employment opportunities in the shipbuilding sector. We need to draw up a National Shipbuilding Plan and ships of the future need to be built in accordance with the Energy Efficiency Design Index approved by the IMO and propelled by environment friendly fuel.

The warship building industry in India is firmly anchored on self-reliance and indigenisation. The Indian Navy set up its naval design directorate in 1964. India built its first indigenous naval warship, a patrol vessel INS *Ajay* in 1961, at Garden Reach Shipyard in Kolkata. Over the past 50 years, our naval designers have designed and our indigenous shipyards have built ships for the Indian Navy resulting in our transformation from a buyer's Navy to a builder's Navy. Today it is a matter of great pride that nearly 50 ships and submarines under construction for the Indian Navy are being built in Indian shipyards, both public and private. These range from aircraft carrier to frigates, destroyers and submarines. It is our endeavour to progressively increase the indigenous content so that future warships and submarines are 100 per cent made in India.

The fishing industry is another sector which provides significant opportunities for growth. India has approximately 2 50,000 fishing boats, with 4 million active fishermen and 14 million people as part of the fishing community. The annual marine fish landings and production in India are over 11.5 million tons which accounts for approximately 5.3 per cent of the world's production. The sector contributes around USD 7 billion to India's foreign exchange earnings and has a potential to grow much more.

However, this is only scratching the surface of the vast potential of the fishing industry in India which is largely coastal in nature, with logistic and maintenance support being provided by local, small-scale enterprises and fishing boats operating in coastal waters. There exists a huge potential for growth in the fishing sector by undertaking deep sea fishing, increasing the size and number of the current fishing fleet and enhancing the support infrastructure for stowage, processing and transporting the catch. The Government has promulgated the National Fishing Policy 2017 with a focus on deep sea fishing and sustainable fishing. Deep sea fishing is another avenue where India could cooperate to harness the Blue Economy. This would also result in coastal community development and enhanced employment opportunities in the fishing sector.

India has over 1,300 Islands and islets as part of the Andaman and

Nicobar Islands and the Lakshadweep Group and Islands off the West and East coasts of India. The Government has prepared a comprehensive plan for the development of the islands, which takes into account aspects of security, economic sustenance, environmental preservation and social and cultural sustenance. This development of the islands will ensure green field infrastructure projects with minimum carbon footprint and opportunities for controlled eco-tourism. Opening of the maritime tourism sector could open up a host of opportunities in the future for development of marinas and cruise tourism. The development of Andaman and Nicobar Islands will enhance the connectivity options with our littoral neighbours in the Bay of Bengal.

India's EEZ also provides offshore energy resources and we have oil and gas exploration areas off the West and East coasts of India. India has also been allocated deep sea bed mining areas in the Central Indian Ocean and these sectors are likely to register significant growth in the coming years.

Renewable ocean energy is another un-harnessed niche sector with immense scope in the future. This includes tidal and wave energy and ocean thermal energy conversion. It can therefore be seen that while there is an ocean of opportunities for development of maritime interests for economic growth, the challenges lie in ensuring that these are greenfield projects, with a minimum impact on the environment, to ensure sustainable development.

While India is focused on economic development of its maritime interests, it is also committed to travelling down the path of sustainable development. The United Nations General Assembly published a document in 2015 titled 'Transforming our World', the 2030 agenda for sustainable development with 17 specific goals and 169 targets. Of these, SDG 14 pertains to the conservation and sustainable use of oceans, seas and marine resources. Towards this, India has submitted its voluntary national review report to the UN on the implementation of Sustainable Development Goals (SDG) in July 2017. A clear agenda has been formulated for promoting the 'Blue Revolution', while charting the way ahead for preventing pollution, an integrated plan for fishing, optimal utilisation of resources with minimum impact on the environment and ensuring sustainable development of the oceans.

The Indian Ocean has emerged as the global economic highway, which is rich in oil and mineral resources. It is the third largest water body spanning an area of 68.5 million sq km and countries on the rim of the ocean are home to nearly one third of humanity.

The seas are no longer a benign medium and globalisation has led to vulnerability of the oceans. The threats and challenges in the maritime domain are as wide and varied as they come and include piracy, maritime terrorism, arms trafficking, drugs smuggling, human trafficking and poaching or IUU fishing. Another challenge is that the waters of the Bay of Bengal and the Indian Ocean are prone to natural disasters and the Navy and Coast Guard have to be ready for rapid response to provide humanitarian assistance and disaster relief.

The instabilities and turbulence on land in some parts of the Indian Ocean have the potential to spill over into the maritime domain and the situation can best be described as 'Fragile'. Consequently, over 120 warships from about 20 navies are always present in the Indian Ocean to safeguard their maritime interests. India has vast maritime interests and the responsibility for protecting these maritime interests fall squarely on the shoulders of the men in white uniform as it is the responsibility of the Navy and the Coast Guard to ensure that our maritime interests, which have a vital relationship with the nation's economic growth, are allowed to develop unhindered at all times.

In 2008, the Indian Navy launched a unique initiative of the Indian Ocean Naval Symposium (IONS) which was a construct to manage the maritime affairs of the countries of the Indian Ocean Region. Over the years, the IONS has emerged as an effective organisation for maritime cooperation. In my view, IONS has the potential to provide an effective template to promote cooperation in the maritime domain in the Indian Ocean Region.

The Indian Ocean Rim Association (IORA) is another organisation which provides the avenue for the strengthening of maritime cooperation between countries of the Indian Ocean Region. Incidentally, 20 members of IORA also have their navies as members of IONS and recent years have witnessed some synergy between IONS and IORA for promoting maritime cooperation.

In order to further promote cooperation among navies of the world, the Indian Navy conducted the International Fleet Review at Vishakhapatnam on the East Coast of India in 2016. Fifty navies of the world came together to strengthen bridges of friendship and we had nearly 100 ships at the review anchorage. The underlying theme of the Review was that we may be separated by geography but are certainly united through the oceans.

During the International Fleet Review, Prime Minister Narendra Modi outlined his vision for the Blue Economy and linked the blue chakra or wheel in our national flag with the potential of the Blue Economy. The Honourable Prime Minister also articulated his maritime vision for the Indian Ocean as SAGAR, which means the ocean and the acronym stands for Security and Growth for all in the Region. India's recent initiatives in the maritime domain, including the quest for harnessing the Blue Economy, are pointers to indicate that India has once again turned towards the seas and is destined to emerge as a resurgent maritime nation.

The Indian Ocean has emerged as the world's centre of gravity in the maritime domain. Another unique feature of the Indian Ocean is that 80 per cent of the oil and trade that emanates in the Indian Ocean is extra-regional in nature. This implies that if there is any impediment in the free flow of oil or trade, it would have a detrimental impact not just on the economies of the region but on the global economy as well. Safety, security and stability on the waters of the Indian Ocean is therefore of paramount importance, and it is the collective responsibility of the navies and the coast guards to ensure the security of the 'global commons'. Networking among navies and global maritime partnerships between countries of the region therefore need to be strengthened in the coming years.

In conclusion, six major aspects require our attention as a nation:

The United Nation's documents 'Transforming Our World—Agenda 2030' and the 'Sustainable Development Goal, SDG 14', provide a template for conservation of the oceans, seas and resources. We now need to outline a perspective plan for sustainable development and growth in different avenues of the maritime sector.

As a maritime nation, India has a significant potential to harness the Blue Economy. We need to chart a national-level maritime policy to harness the Blue Economy for sustained development of the oceans.

There is a requirement for an apex-level organisation to coordinate and integrate the planning process of various departments and agencies in the maritime domain for economic development of our maritime interests and implementing Blue Economy initiatives so as to enable India to emerge as a resurgent maritime nation.

The Indian Ocean Naval Symposium (IONS) and the Indian Ocean Rim Association (IORA) are important maritime constructs to manage the maritime affairs of the IOR. There needs to be greater synergy between IONS and IORA to enhance maritime cooperation between countries of the Indian Ocean Region.

To fully implement the Honourable Prime Minister's vision of SAGAR, that is, 'Security and Growth for All In the Region', we need to draw up a detailed roadmap for maritime cooperation with various countries of the region with a 'whole-of-government approach' so as to shape a positive and favourable maritime environment in the Indian Ocean Region.

The Honourable Prime Minister has launched a dynamic initiative of Swachh Bharat (Clean India). We need to extend the concept to Swachh Sagar (Clean and Healthy Oceans). This could be a people's movement where we draw up an action plan and motivate every citizen and maritime agencies to contribute towards cleaning our coastal areas and extend the initiative to our littoral neighbours to ensure clean and healthy oceans or 'Swachh Sagar' for future generations.

The seas around us are gaining new-found importance as each day goes by because of their linkages with the Blue Economy and I have no doubt that the current century is the century of the seas. There is no doubt that our future economic well-being rests on our ability to harness the Blue Economy, ensure maritime security of the seas around us, enhance maritime cooperation between the countries in the region and ensure sustainable development of the oceans.

9

Leveraging the UN for a Comprehensive Convention on International Terrorism

Asoke Mukerji

Why the UN?

The United Nations (UN) is the only universal platform for a rule of law-based response to counter terrorism. All 193-member states of the UN have signed the treaty known as the UN Charter. This obliges them to uphold the principles of the Charter, including the obligations assumed by them in accordance with the Charter. Under Article 13 of the Charter, member-states are committed to promoting international cooperation through legal measures. The Comprehensive Convention on International Terrorism (CCIT) should be seen in this context. Once adopted, the CCIT will become an international framework to counter all forms of terrorism, including the trans-border activities of terrorists and terrorist entities.

The issue of countering terrorism was not included in the UN Charter signed in 1945. The UN began to act seriously against international terrorism only after the September 1972 terror attack that killed 11 Israeli athletes during the Munich Olympics. The United

Nations General Assembly (UNGA) adopted a resolution on countering terrorism on 18 December 1972. This resolution established an Ad Hoc Committee on International Terrorism.

The Committee consisted of 35 countries, including India. Its mandate was to discuss the need for a multilateral legal framework to counter-terrorism. By 1979, the Committee, chaired by India, submitted its report to the UNGA. The report included a proposal for the negotiation of an additional international convention, or conventions, based "on the principle of extradition or prosecution to combat acts of international terrorism not yet covered by other similar international conventions".

The UNGA asked the UN Secretary General, based on views of the member-states conveyed in the Ad Hoc Committee, to follow up on this proposal. The core issue was of extraditing for prosecution or prosecuting, those accused of the crime of terrorism. It was clear that effective action to counter terrorism depended on integrating this principle into a comprehensive international legal instrument by the United Nations. Due to Cold War politics, the proposal was not taken further until 1994.

In 1994, the UNGA unanimously adopted a resolution, which reiterated its commitment to counter terrorism, including through the principle of extraditing or prosecuting perpetrators of terrorist acts. This was followed up by the establishment of an Ad Hoc Committee on Measures to Eliminate International Terrorism, open to all member-states, by another unanimous UNGA resolution in 1997. The mandate given to the Committee was to draft international legal instruments to counter terrorist bombings, suppress acts of nuclear terrorism, and develop "a comprehensive legal framework of conventions dealing with international terrorism". A Declaration annexed to this Resolution placed emphasis on the principle of extraditing or prosecuting perpetrators of terrorist acts.

In November 1996, India took the initiative to circulate a "first draft" of a CCIT. Within the Ad Hoc Committee, however, it was decided to keep this draft in abeyance until the sectoral negotiations on the Convention on Suppression of Terrorist Bombings and the

Convention on the Suppression of Financing of Terrorism were completed. Work on the CCIT was pushed back further when the Ad Hoc Committee decided to complete work on a Convention on Suppression of Acts of Nuclear Terrorism, eventually adopted in 2005.

In 2005, the 6th Committee of the UNGA, on the recommendation of the Ad Hoc Committee, established a Working Group to move the CCIT forward. Dr. Rohan Perera of Sri Lanka, who had successfully steered the negotiations of the Ad Hoc Committee in the three sectoral conventions on terrorist bombings, financing of terrorism and nuclear terrorism, was elected Chairman of the Working Group. So far, the Working Group has been unable to harvest the CCIT.

Reasons for the Logjam

The main issues of divergence today among the participants in the Ad Hoc Committee on the drafting of a CCIT are well known. There are four major areas. These relate to excluding acts by "national liberation movements", which is linked to the issue of the "definition" of terrorism, from the scope of the CCIT. The Organisation of the Islamic Conference (OIC) has adopted an uncompromising stance on this issue. This is linked with the OIC position on the Palestine Liberation Organisation (PLO), which does not fall under the definition of a terrorist organisation. A second issue relates to the demand by several left-wing Latin American countries to include "state terrorism" in the CCIT. This issue is linked to the perception that several regimes in Latin America were using state forces to quell popular left-wing movements, like the Sandinistas in Nicaragua. A third issue relates to the demand by some countries to exclude the acts of national armed forces during peacetime from the CCIT's coverage. Separately, Egypt has called for a UN High Level Conference to formulate a joint organised response to terrorism.

The Working Group's efforts have continued for more than a decade. The draft text of the CCIT (with its unresolved issues) has been on the table since 2007. This draft contains several provisions elaborating on the issue of "prosecute or extradite". In April 2013, the Working Group considered a proposal to address the outstanding issues by incorporating them in a UNGA resolution when adopting the CCIT as a purely legal instrument to deal with the crime of terrorism. This proposal has not been agreed to by the member-states. At a meeting of the 6th Committee of the UNGA in November 2015, Dr. Rohan Perera reported that despite attempts to propose compromise language on the contentious issues, the position of countries remained divergent. He said that these issues were of a "political, rather than legal, nature".

Resolving the Differences

The UNGA has a track record of addressing and resolving contentious issues. In the case of the CCIT, the UNGA should adopt the legal Convention without bringing in the political issues. Simultaneously, the UNGA can adopt a "political" resolution to reflect the priorities of member-states on countering terrorism. Of course, it is the CCIT as a legal instrument which will be relevant in any measure taken by UN member-states which are party to the Convention on Counter Terrorism.

The current situation in international relations would appear to favour this approach. The member-states most active in this issue are those from the OIC, the USA, the European Union, the Russian Federation, Latin American member-states such as Nicaragua, and India. In recent years, the impact of international terrorism has been felt across the world, especially in Africa. Countries like Libya, Mali, Nigeria, Uganda, Sudan, Ethiopia, Somalia and Kenya have suffered from these increased terrorist attacks and would participate actively in the Working Group. The objective should be to discuss and agree on the way forward within the framework proposed by Dr. Rohan Perera.

Issues of Extradition

The need to extradite alleged terrorists if a member-state cannot or will not prosecute them is, of course, the key to the CCIT's relevance. For India, this is a priority. We all know who the terrorists were who planned the heinous terrorist attack on Mumbai on 26 November 2008. We also know where they are located. If the UN member-state, where these persons are located, does not prosecute them, then the CCIT will oblige that member-state to extradite these persons for prosecution to a jurisdiction where they can be prosecuted. In practice, once the CCIT has been adopted, member-states will adopt enabling legislation to make it effective in their national jurisdictions. This would include extradition arrangements with other member-states which are party to the CCIT.

A new dimension to the issue of extradition arrangements which is becoming important is the integration of digital means to implement extradition agreements. The existing framework of Mutual Legal Assistance Treaties (MLATs) is slowly being upgraded to electronic MLATS. This will have a positive impact on the proposed CCIT.

A likely barrier to extradition arrangements can come from the Permanent Members of the UN Security Council (UNSC). These five countries (China, France, Russia, the UK and the USA) have become accustomed to using the consensus on a global fight against terrorism to inject their political priorities as UNSC members into efforts by the Security Council to counter terrorism. These five countries can do so because they control the decision-making process within the UNSC. Article 27.3 of the UN Charter gives them the right to reject any decisions proposed for the UNSC by not giving their "concurrence". This is known popularly as the right to veto.

Since the mid-1990s the UNSC has adopted a series of resolutions to counter terrorism. Under Article 24 of the UN Charter, the "primary responsibility" for the maintenance of international peace and security has been delegated by the member-states of the United Nations to the UNSC. As the impact of international terrorism has continued to spread, posing a direct threat to international peace and security, the UNSC has responded by adopting resolutions under Chapter VII of the Charter to counter this threat.

The UNSC is authorised under Article 41 of the UN Charter to consider "measures not involving the use of armed force" to give effect to its decisions. Under Article 25 of the Charter, all members of the United Nations have agreed to "accept and carry out the decisions" of the UNSC.

The ineffectiveness of the UNSC to counter terrorism is due to two factors. One is the overt politicisation of its approach to countering terrorism, which undercuts the "rule-of-law" approach. The second is the ineffectiveness of the UNSC to enforce its own decisions on the ground, including by enforcing sanctions imposed by its resolutions. This requires reform of the UNSC, as unanimously agreed to by all the world leaders at the 60th anniversary summit of the UN in 2005.

The preferred approach of the major UNSC resolutions to counter terrorism has been to condemn terror acts, recall obligations of member-states to fight against terrorism, including the concept of "zero tolerance" of terrorism, offer support for capacity building in member-states to counter terrorism, and introduce sanctions in specific cases if the five Permanent Members are in agreement. The objective of obliging member-states to prosecute or extradite for prosecution alleged terrorists has not yet been part of UNSC resolutions on countering terrorism. No major UNSC Resolution on countering terrorism, for example, has so far incorporated the principle of "extradite or prosecute" in its course of action.

Take the case of UNSC Resolution 1267, which is where many terrorists or terrorist entities posing a direct threat to India are listed. The Preamble of UNSC Resolution 1267, adopted in 1999 to deal with the threat posed by Al-Qaida and associated individuals and entities, did recall the obligations of parties to "existing" international counter-terrorism conventions to "extradite or prosecute terrorists". However, in the absence of a CCIT, no "existing" international convention places obligations on UN member-states to give effect to the principle of "extradite or prosecute" to counter terrorism. The course of action mandated by Resolution 1267 does not include extradition or prosecution.

The fact that UNSC resolutions are essentially political in nature was clear when the UNSC split Resolution 1267 in 2011 into two separate UNSC resolutions (UNSC Resolution 1988 to focus on the Taliban and UNSC Resolution 1989 to focus on Al-Qaida). This was done to provide political flexibility to reintegrate elements of the Taliban listed earlier with Al-Qaida under UNSC Resolution 1267 into the Afghan peace process.

Even UNSC Resolution 1373, perhaps the most significant response of the UNSC to counter terrorism adopted after the 9/11 terror attacks on the USA, does not refer at all to any obligation of member-states of the UN to extradite or prosecute perpetrators of terrorist acts.

The UNSC has so far failed to protect UN personnel deployed by it from terrorist acts. The kidnapping of Filipino and Fijian UN peacekeepers of UNDOF, deployed under UNSC Resolution 350 in 1974 in the Golan Heights in two separate incidents in 2014 by the Al-Nusra terrorist group, was widely reported by the international media as well as by the UN. Similarly, more than 100 UN peacekeepers, mainly from Africa, have been killed in Mali by terrorists affiliated with Al Shabab, which is in the UNSC sanctions list. The response of the UNSC to this direct challenge to its authority by a terrorist group listed in the sanctions list remains unknown, despite calls during UNSC open debates to ask member-states to investigate, prosecute and penalize terrorist groups involved in these incidents in order to deter terrorism.

In September 2014, faced with growing evidence of the rapid spread of terrorism and the movement of terrorists across borders, the UNSC adopted Resolution 2178 on "foreign terrorist fighters". Paragraph 6 of this Resolution refers to the need for member-states to "prosecute and to penalize" terrorists, but omits to mention the need for a supportive international legal framework necessary for member-states to sustain this action, including through international cooperation on extradition. In the Resolution's section on "International Cooperation", for example, there is no reference to the requirement to "extradite or prosecute" foreign terrorist fighters. The absence of a CCIT makes this omission possible.

India must prioritize the adoption of the CCIT by the UNGA as it is an elected member of the UNSC from January 2021. Its objective should be to make the CCIT a normative framework for UNSC resolutions on countering terrorism, requiring member-states to prosecute or extradite for prosecution alleged terrorists.

India's Role

India can use the opportunity to overcome the deadlock on the CCIT during the next UNGA review of the UN Global Counter Terrorism Strategy (GCTS), which was formulated and adopted on 8 September 2006. The review takes place every two years, with the next one due in 2022. The GCTS rests on four pillars. These are addressing conditions conducive to the spread of terrorism; measures to prevent and combat terrorism; measures to build states' capacity to prevent and combat terrorism and to strengthen the role of the UN in that regard; and measures to ensure respect of human rights for all and the rule of law as the fundamental basis for the fight against terrorism.

The focus in the UNGA since 2006 has been on implementing the GCTS. Even in this framework, though the "principle to extradite or prosecute" features under the fourth pillar of the Plan of Action of the GCTS, little progress has been registered, let alone concerted action taken, to conclude the CCIT. One priority for India would be to have the UNGA agree on a deadline in the review of the GCTS for concluding negotiations on the CCIT. The structural reform within the UN Secretariat of bringing all 38 UN entities involved in implementing the GCTS under an Under Secretary General since June 2017 should be integrated by India in this context. A Russian national has been appointed by the UN Secretary General as the first incumbent of this post.

A second initiative that India can take in the UN is to use its membership as an elected member of the UNSC for 2021-22 to push for greater synergy between the UN and other organisations outside the UN to help set norms and enforce the rule of law to counter terrorism. Already, the UNSC has begun to adopt such an approach. India has announced its intention to prioritize activity in the UNSC on this.

An area that is visible is the synergy between the UNSC and the Financial Action Task Force (FATF). The FATF was created initially by the G-7 Summit held in Paris in 1989 to address the issue of money laundering. The FATF is serviced by the secretariat of the Organisation for Economic Cooperation and Development (OECD) in Paris to issue recommendations on this issue.

In 2001, the FATF was given the mandate to develop recommendations to counter terrorist financing. It may be noted that this mandate was given after the UNGA, which includes all the members of FATF, had already adopted the legally negotiated universal International Convention for the Suppression of Financing of Terrorism in 1999. Today, the FATF has 34 countries (including India, which joined in 2010) as its members.

All the five Permanent Members of the UNSC are members of FATF. The UNSC has incorporated FATF recommendations into UNSC Resolution 1267 adopted in 1999 to counter the terrorist threat posed by Al Qaida and the Taliban; UNSC Resolution 1373 adopted in 2001 after the 9/11 terror attack on the USA; UNSC Resolution 1540 adopted in 2004 on non-proliferation of weapons of mass destruction; UNSC Resolution 1718 adopted in 2006 on non-proliferation and the DPR of Korea as well as UNSC Resolution 1737 adopted the same year on non-proliferation. Of the FATF recommendations on international cooperation, Recommendation 39 upholds the principle of either extraditing or prosecuting perpetrators of terrorism financing, which, of course, limits the application of this principle to other acts of terrorism.

India's focus on countering terrorism sponsored by Pakistan directed against India has benefited from the FATF-UNSC synergy. Apart from placing member-states like Pakistan in the list of countries that need to take effective action against the financing of terrorism, the FATF also enables enforcement of its norms using the network of financial institutions that are part of the jurisdiction of FATF member-states, which gives a global reach to such enforcement.

A second platform which can be synergized with the UNSC is the Global Counter Terrorism Forum (GCTF), of which India is a founder-member since it was established in Washington DC in 2011. UNSC Resolution 2178 has brought in the GCTF's norm-setting work to which India has contributed to the effort to enforce the UN's counter terrorism activity.

The GCTF, initiated by the USA in 2011, originated in the Counter Terrorism Action Group (CTAG), established by the G-8 Summit in

Evian, France, in 2003 as a reaction to the way the UNSC was countering terrorism. To broaden the impact of CTAG, the USA, supported by some other G-8 members, created the GCTF, with 30 countries (including India) as founder members.

All five Permanent Members of the UNSC are members of the GCTF. The GCTF's Rabat Memorandum on Good Practices for Effective Counterterrorism Practice in the Criminal Justice Sector deals with the issue of extradition. Good Practice 9 calls for international cooperation, including extradition, but does not refer to the principle of "extradite or prosecute". Interestingly, not only the GCTF Good Practices for Effective Counterterrorism Practice, but the entire corpus of the normative work done by the GCTF so far has been incorporated by specific references into the UNSC Resolution 2178 on foreign terrorist fighters.

Challenges to Declaring Pakistan a 'Rogue State'

There does not appear to be any coordinated attempt in the UN to declare Pakistan a rogue state. There are individuals and entities in Pakistan who are sought for committing terrorist acts against Pakistan's neighbours such as India and Afghanistan. China has used or rather mis-used its privilege as a Permanent Member of the UNSC to "block" action on India's requests to list individuals accused of fomenting terrorism directed against India in the UNSC sanctions list. The most recent example of China's use of this "hidden veto" as a Permanent Member was the case of Masood Azhar. It took several years to overcome the "block" put by China for listing in the UNSC sanctions list.

The UN's attempt to counter such individuals and entities raises two issues. One is the responsibility of Pakistan as a member-state of the UN, which is after all based on its treaty obligations under the UN Charter. The UN needs to see how member-states fulfil their legal obligations under the Charter not to allow their territories to be used for violating the principles of the Charter, which include non-use of force against the territorial integrity or political independence of UN member-states like India.

The other element is the increasing reference by member-states that terrorist acts are being committed by non-state actors. This implies that member-states do not have any responsibility for the actions of such non-state actors. However, if the member-state is sovereign and in control of its territory and is a party to the treaty (UN Charter), then it cannot absolve itself of its sovereign rights and responsibilities. It must act against non-state actors that are on its territory, or on territory which is controlled by its state institutions like the armed forces. The UNGA and the UNSC need to take more effective measures to make this clear to all member-states.

The UNSC and the UN must demonstrate the effectiveness of the multilateral system to counter terrorism within the framework of the legal conventions on countering terrorism, and the numerous obligations placed by UNSC resolutions on countering terrorism. That includes a review of how to enforce these conventions and resolutions. That is a major challenge for the objective of reformed multilateralism.

10

India and the Evolving Global Security Landscape

Sujan R. Chinoy

Introduction

The dawn of this century, particularly the year 2001, stood out for accelerated globalisation in trade and investment following China's entry into the WTO, and the primacy accorded to national security following the terrorist attacks on US territory on 11 September. The past two decades have witnessed the rise of China, the fracturing of power, the ability of state and non-state actors to overcome gaps in conventional power through asymmetrical means and the increasing hybridisation of conflicts. For nations around the world, these have brought together a cascading mélange of traditional and non-traditional security challenges such as economic and military competition, climate change, cyber threats, terrorism, and food and energy security. International security, already a complex web of inter-related threats, is now acquiring new dimensions.

The global situation has witnessed a rapid flux, with geo-political and economic contestations creating profound uncertainty. Key drivers of globalisation have experienced stress. International relations are increasingly marked by a proclivity to 'weaponise' trade and technology. An inward-looking USA under President Trump was trying to retain its position at the top of the international order while rejecting multilateralism. This had weakened the United Nations and its agencies such as UNESCO, the WTO, the Paris Agreement on Climate Change, and trans-Atlantic and trans-Pacific partnerships. China, on the other hand, is determined to preserve the gains of a liberal trading order and canvas for a global endorsement of its systems of political governance and economic development. Erosion of US primacy in global political, economic and military affairs is an abiding Chinese objective.

Under Prime Minister Narendra Modi, India has deftly maintained good relations with the USA and Russia, Saudi Arabia and Iran and Israel and the Arab nations, their differences notwithstanding. India has maintained robust postures on its borders with China whenever necessary. Strategic ties have been enhanced with the USA, France, Japan and several other countries. Close personal relations between Modi and the leaders of Gulf nations have translated into closer intelligence sharing. India is destined to play a key role in the evolving security and economic architecture in the Indo-Pacific.

Today, the fragile international compact has been rendered a huge blow by COVID-19,—a fast-spreading and silent killer—which quickly spread from China to the rest of the world, acquiring mutants along the way. The pandemic has exposed flaws in multi-lateral structures and highlighted the lacunae in national capacities, particularly in healthcare.[1]

Multilateralism has suffered retrenchment.[2] The UN Security Council must be faulted for its egregious lack of action in March 2020 when China held the rotating post of President. It will remain one of the great ironies of history that China, which has increasingly sought to play a global leadership role, actively suppressed discussions in the face of a monumental threat to the lives and security of millions around the world. The withdrawal of nearly USD 500 million of annual voluntary funding by the USA to the World Health Organisation (WHO) was a debatable move, notwithstanding the global consensus on the WHO's questionable conduct and Chinabias.[3] The Biden

Administration has engaged in course correction from its very first day in office.

The daily information overload about the pandemic created a surreal atmosphere within homes and in public places under lockdowns that spared few. Quotidian routines of work, leisure and human contact have been disrupted in myriad unrecognisable ways. Workers around the world, whether in government or the private sector, are obliged to function from home, leading to a surge in users and data flow in digital space. This has created vast new attack surfaces in personal computers for hackers and cyber criminals, both state and non-state, to exploit. The very notion of critical infrastructure in the cyber domain is changing with growing dependence on webinars and online tasks, including for hospitals, banks and providers of essential services.

COVID-19: India Can Lead

Yet, the rapid spread of coronavirus around the world has created fresh opportunities for dialogue.[4] There is hope and scope for creating a new global compact. Contributions will be measured not in dollars and cents alone but in the leadership that countries exhibit and their willingness to share ideas, best practices and available resources to develop an international mechanism for monitoring, verification, early warning and cooperation among nation-states. Such a framework will have to look beyond the limitations of the controversial WHO.[5]

India's ancient civilisation has given much to the world, among which Buddha's teachings of peace and non-violence stand out. Mahatma Gandhi's advocacy of a non-violent struggle for India's independence still resonates around the world. Gandhi also spoke of moderation in the abuse of the Earth's limited resources. He famously said that the Earth has enough to meet the needs of each one of us, but not our greed. Prime Minister Narendra Modi is a staunch believer in the natural harmony that should exist between humans and Mother Nature. One paragraph in particular stands out in his acceptance speech on 3 October 2018 when the UN bestowed on him the Champions of the Earth Award[6]:

> *"Today, human society stands at an important crossroads. The path that we take hereon will not only determine our well-being but also that of the generations who will inhabit our planet after us. The imbalances between our greed and necessities have led to grave ecological imbalances. We can either accept this, go ahead with things as if it is business as usual, or we can take corrective actions."*

Prime Minister Modi's recollection, in the same address, of the Doctrine of Trusteeship propounded by Gandhi that we are custodians of the Earth which we must bestow in a good shape to future generations, was a timely reminder to a world accustomed to unbridled consumption of every kind.

This is particularly true as we endeavour to create a new cohort for cooperation in dealing with not just the COVID-19 pandemic but also the uncertainties surrounding economic growth, healthcare and food security in a post-COVID-19 era. This is especially relevant since difficulties are bound to mount as a result of the economic cost of the pandemic. Developing countries, in particular, will find it the hardest to fulfil their aspirations.

The principle of non-violence or "ahimsa", holds a special place in Indian culture. Vegetarianism in India has its basis in religious beliefs and in the theory of *karma*, but also flows from a genuine respect for all sentient beings. It is neither necessary nor feasible to impose vegetarianism on those with different belief systems and culinary traditions. However, in the light of COVID-19, there definitely exists a case for greater scrutiny of "wet markets" in China, South-East Asia, and in many other countries around the world.[7] From tigers, monkeys, donkeys and pangolins to snakes, bats, geckos and monitor lizards, all have been subjected to illegal poaching and trafficking in all parts around the world. Culinary traditions are a function of culture as well as geographical and climatic conditions. In the north-east of India, for example, it is a common practice for the local people to consume many of the animals that are associated with "wet markets". Roadside quacks across South Asia are seen extolling the spurious curative powers of lizard oils and other extracts of protected species. Even the USA, which has enacted the Endangered Species Act in 1973, has not been able to eradicate animal farms that breed and trade in exotic species. China operates commercial tiger farms for traditional medicine and South-East Asia does likewise with bears for bile extraction. All these activities increase the potential for zoonotic transmission of unknown and deadly viruses.

The need of the hour is to devise means that can deal more effectively with the illegal slaughter of exotic animals for bush meat and the use of animal extracts for traditional medicine. Efforts must be made to strengthen the Convention on International Trade in Endangered Species of Wild Fauna and Flora (CITES), a multilateral treaty with more than 180 member-countries. There should be renewed focus not only on the illegal international trade that is already covered by CITES but also the hazardous exploitation of exotic wildlife species within national borders. All signatory states, including China, must pass and enforce legislation to control the domestic consumption of wild animals. Dubious "wet markets" and animal farms must be shut down.[8]

India's record of legislation in conservation and enforcement of penalties for the killing and exploitation of protected wildlife is better than most. There is considerable scope for the Modi government to take the lead in proposing that CITES be given more teeth to conduct international scrutiny and inspections.

Today, at a strategic level, global opinion seems weighted against China, notwithstanding its efforts to salvage credibility by shifting the focus away from the origins of the coronavirus to the "superiority" of its system in tackling the pandemic. There is fresh speculation of the coronavirus having originated in a laboratory in Wuhan, with theories abounding about biological warfare programmes and accidental release. This provides an opportune moment to turn the spotlight to the inherent weaknesses of the Biological Weapons Convention (BWC) of 1975. It is a disarmament treaty that does not prohibit the retention and use of biological agents, including corona viruses, for prophylactic purposes which encompass medical research for diagnosis and immunisation. It has no verification protocol to deal with any suspected use of biological agents. Indeed, the UN Security Council can investigate complaints in this regard, but the veto power enjoyed by the Permanent Members, including China, renders this a chimera. In the run-up to the 9th Review Conference of the BWC in 2021, India could engage in consultations with other middle powers to evolve a regime that can provide better oversight.[9]

The COVID-19 pandemic, meanwhile, has brought across a home truth: that wealth is unable to protect even the most affluent people from a silent killer. As Mahatma Gandhi said, "It is health that is real wealth and not pieces of gold and silver".[10] Individuals with higher immunity levels have a better chance of survival if afflicted with COVID-19. The ancient Indian practice of Yoga is known to boost immunity levels through the cultivation of a healthy mind and body. This is the time to further reinforce the worldwide practice of Yoga under the banner of the International Day of Yoga which was also an initiative of Prime Minister Modi. India should plan for special virtual events on June 21 to encourage people around the world to practise Yoga as a means to promote holistic health.

As the world's largest producer and exporter of cost-effective generic drugs,[11] India's readiness to ship the anti-malarial drug, hydroxychloroquinine, to fight COVID-19 to others was a "good Samaritan" act in consonance with the ethos of *Vasudheva Kutumbakam*. India s sent rapid response teams to several countries. It also conducted research to produce a vaccine. If China is a "factory to the world", India has to live up to its reputation to be a "pharmacy to the world". It can take on a new and well-deserved moniker, that of *Vishwa Vaidya* (global physician).[12] This provides an opportunity to promote Ayurveda, which complements Yoga.

At a time when the UNSC, G20, G7 and the EU were inert, Prime Minister Modi stood out with his initiatives to develop a joint response.[13] He convened a teleconference with SAARC nations on 15 March 2020. A SAARC COVID-19 Emergency Fund for rapid regional response, including pooling healthcare resources, was the key outcome of this conference.[14] Modi announced an initial contribution of USD 10 million for the Fund.[15] His initiative was hailed by countries such as the USA, Russia and many others. Since then, despite the great task of providing healthcare for its 1.3 billion people, India has despatched rapid response teams of specialists as well as medical equipment to several countries. India has also imparted online training to emergency response staff. Other Indian initiatives include the use of the SAARC Disaster Management Centre to exchange best practices.[16] First off the block in promoting regional cooperation, India had announced a network training programme on COVID-19 for healthcare professionals of SAARC countries.[17] As Modi said, *"Our neighbourhood collaboration should be a model for the world"*.[18]

Similarly, Modi's proposal for cooperation among G20 countries led to an Extraordinary Virtual G20 Leaders' Summit on 26 March 2020 to discuss the challenges posed by the outbreak and to forge a coordinated global response. During this meeting, Modi underscored the need for "reformed multilateralism", one that would put human beings at the centre of India's vision of global prosperity and cooperation, freely and openly share the benefits of medical research and development, develop adaptive, responsive and humane health care systems, promote new crisis management protocols and procedures for an interconnected global village, strengthen and reform intergovernmental organisations like the WHO, and work together to reduce economic hardships resulting from COVID-19, particularly for the economically weak.[19] He urged global leaders to usher in a new globalisation for the collective well-being of humankind and have a multilateral focus on promoting the shared interests of humanity even when globalisation had failed in many ways.[20] Both Prime Minister Modi and Minister of External Affairs S. Jaishankar have been remarkably active in engaging counterparts from around the world to tackle the pandemic.

Underpinnings of India's Approach to International Security

India has witnessed an all-round transformation in recent years. The downturn in economic growth triggered by the COVID-19 pandemic poses a serious challenge. However, when viewed through a longer-term prism, the world is still likely to bet on India emerging stronger from the current crisis. India's strong democratic traditions, its youthful demography and institutionalised political stability can still propel it into a higher orbit in the future.

Today, India is no longer a passive observer of world affairs, nor simply a follower. It is capable of engaging an anxiety-ridden world that is caught in a pandemic against the backdrop of ideological battles and trade wars. India is capable of playing a leadership role in bringing the world together to practise a new and reformed version of multilateralism which places the common benefit of humanity above narrow national interests, particularly in healthcare. It is poised to emerge as a strong pillar in the Indo-Pacific, contributing to a strengthened and more reliable multi-polar order in the post COVID-19 period.

As Modi has outlined earlier, India will be guided by the values of *Samman* (respect), *Samvad* (dialogue), *Sahayog* (cooperation), *Shanti* (peace) and *Samriddhi* (prosperity).[21]

Synergistic Exercise of Soft and Hard Power

The assessment that India is better known for its "soft power" must be leavened with a realistic assessment of Indian foreign, defence and national security policies which also feature accretion in "hard power" and political resolve to take recourse to it if need be. Under Prime Minister Modi, India has demonstrated a capacity for bold initiatives and decisions. There is a greater willingness to take calculated risks. This calls for the world to recalibrate its policies towards India. The "New India" simply cannot be taken for granted by either friend or foe.

In recent years, India has taken the lead in shaping the global agenda. Countering terrorism, particularly cross-border terrorism emanating from Pakistan, remains a core national priority. Long a victim of terrorism, India has now in place policies and options for retaliation based on "zero tolerance" for terrorism, as seen in the bold cross-border surgical strikes and air strikes against Pakistan in 2016 and 2019, respectively. India is actively contributing to consensus building in the Global Counter Terrorism Forum (GCTF) and the Financial Action Task Force (FATF), including on terror financing. There is growing support for India's proposal for a "Comprehensive Convention on International Terrorism" (CCIT). Barring a few countries that obfuscate the definition of terrorism for vested interests, the large majority of nations, including the Permanent Members of the UN, have voiced support for expeditious conclusion of such a convention.

Being a peninsula country with vast maritime interests in the Indo-Pacific, India has played a key role in promoting maritime security. It has used its considerable naval and airlift capabilities to conduct humanitarian assistance and disaster relief operations (HADR), particularly to help the Maldives,[22] Sri Lanka[23] and Indonesia,[24] besides conducting joint patrolling of the Exclusive Economic Zone (EEZ) with the first two island neighbours. India has played an active role in conducting anti-piracy operations in the Gulf of Aden[25] and in hosting the Information Fusion Centre-Indian Ocean Region (IFC-IOR) for White Shipping.[26] India conducts bilateral and multilateral maritime exercises with partners on the high seas in support of openness, unimpeded commerce and the freedoms of navigation and over flight.

Another area where India has made a major contribution over the decades is in the field of disarmament and non-proliferation of weapons of mass destruction (WMDs). India's proliferation record remains unblemished. Its principled opposition to the discriminatory Treaty on the Non-Proliferation of Nuclear Weapons (NPT) and the inadequate Comprehensive Test Ban Treaty (CTBT) flows from its belief that neither is a goal in itself and that both have done little to achieve universal and complete nuclear disarmament in a time-bound manner. Under Modi, India has already been admitted as a full member of three of the four major export control regimes. These include the Missile Technology Control Regime (MTCR) in 2016, the Wassenaar Arrangement in 2017 and the Australia Group in 2018. But for China's chronic opposition, India would have been readily admitted to the Nuclear Suppliers Group (NSG). India has traditionally tabled four draft resolutions at the UN on 'Convention on the Prohibition of the Use of Nuclear Weapons', 'Reducing Nuclear Danger', 'Measures to Prevent Terrorists from Acquiring Weapons of Mass Destruction' and 'Role of Science and Technology in the Context of International Security and Disarmament'.[27]

India's contributions at the UN include participation in diverse UN Peace Keeping Operations over the decades. It has also strengthened the developmental impulse through transparent infrastructure and connectivity projects, particularly in South Asia, Africa and Central Asia.

Beyond traditional threats to international security, India has acquitted itself well in tackling climate change and cementing clean energy partnerships around the world. The establishment of the International Solar Alliance, a joint initiative of India and France, and the clarion call by PM Modi for an international Coalition for Disaster Resilient Infrastructure, stand out. In cyber security, India and the USA must redouble their efforts to push for a multi-stakeholder model of Internet governance. This is especially relevant at a time when cybercrime and malicious attacks by state and non-state actors and threats to critical infrastructure are on the rise. Post COVID-19, there will be even greater reliance on artificial intelligence (AI), surveillance technologies, online platforms and big data.

Conclusion

The outline of the post-COVID-19 era, particularly in relation to economic recovery, healthcare and food security, is far from clear. In the long run, there cannot be any clear-cut winner without good health for all in a globalised world. In the proximate future, however, it appears that China is making the fastest recovery, the dubious origins of the corona virus in Wuhan notwithstanding. The pandemic has served to accentuate the rift between the USA and China, with a bi-partisan consensus emerging in domestic US politics on outlook towards China. However, given the inexorable centrality of the Chinese economy in global supply chains, it is clear that the economies of the USA, EU, Japan or even India cannot achieve a major decoupling without inviting supply chain distress upon themselves. COVID-19 has shown how China's actions impact the entire world. Whatever the denouement in the matter of bringing China to book for its acts of commission or omission, its cooperation will be vital in reforming global institutions and practices.

India enjoys good relations with multiple powers and is well-regarded across the developing world. With excellent long-term economic prospects in the decades ahead, India should do its utmost to contain the pandemic and prepare itself to reengage a post-pandemic world that is likely to witness greater trade competition and ideological contestation. There is no room for despair. Despite hardships, India can, and must, take the lead in bringing the world together to practice a new multilateralism which places the common interests of humanity above narrow national interests.

As Prime Minister Modi said at the Shangri La Dialogue in 2018, India will be an enabling, law-abiding, pluralistic and stabilising power in the Indo-Pacific, working in loose concert with the widest possible arc of stakeholders, based on common principles and best practices, to create equitable and sustainable security architecture for the 21st century. The post COVID-19 era is even more likely to feature an Asian Century, and India will definitely have a major role to play as it unfolds.

NOTES

1. Sujan R. Chinoy, "India can absorb shocks of pandemic, take the lead in reshaping global order", *The Indian Express*, May 4, 2020 at https://indianexpress.com/article/opinion/columns/covid-19-pandemic-unsc-china-coronavirus-global-cases-india-lockdowm-sujan-r-chinoy-6392238/
2. Ibid.
3. Ibid.
4. Ibid.
5. Ibid.
6. Modi, N., "In Harmony with Mother Nature", *The Hindu*, October 4, 2018 at https://www.thehindu.com/opinion/op-ed/in-harmony-with-mother-nature/article25115350.ece (Accessed April 18, 2020).
7. Ibid (1).
8. Ibid (1).
9. Ibid (1).
10. Gandhi, M. K. (1948), *Keys to Health*, Ahmedabad: Navjivan Publishing House.
11. "India biggest producer of 'game-changer' hydroxychloroquine drug; has enough capacity", *Live Mint*, April 7, 2020 at https://www.livemint.com/science/health/india-biggest-producer-of-game-changer-hydroxychloroquine-drug-has-enough-capacity-11586266119087.html (Accessed April 18, 2020).
12. Ibid (1).
13. Ibid (1).

14. Ministry of External Affairs (2020), Government of India, "PM interacts with SAARC leaders to combat COVID-19 in the region", March 15, 2020 at https://mea.gov.in/press-releases.htm?dtl/32539/PM_interacts_ with_ SAARC_ leaders_to_combat_COVID19_in_the_region (Accessed April 18, 2020).
15. Ibid.
16. Ibid.
17. Ibid and ITEC Twitter, April 14, 2020 at https://twitter.com/ITECnetwork (Accessed April 18, 2020).
18. Ibid.
19. Ministry of External Affairs (2020), Government of India, "Press Release on the Extraordinary Virtual G20 Leaders' Summit", March 26, 2020 at https://mea.gov.in/press-releases.htm?dtl/32600/Press_Release_on_the_ Extraordinary_Virtual_G20_Leaders_Summit (Accessed April 18, 2020); Ministry of External Affairs (2020), Government of India, "Prime Minister addresses the G20 Virtual Summit, 2020 from New Delhi", March 26, 2020 at https://mea.gov.in/newsdetail1.htm?8036/Prime-Minister-addresses-the-G20-Virtual-Summit-2c-2020-from-New-Delhi- (Accessed April 18, 2020).
20. Ibid.
21. Press Information Bureau (2018), "Text of Prime Minister's Keynote Address at Shangri La Dialogue", June 1, 2018 at https://pib.gov.in/newsite/PrintRelease.aspx?relid=179711 (Accessed April 18, 2020).
22. "Medical Evacuation at Maldives on 25 and 26 February 2018", *Indian Navy,* February 26, 2018 at https://www.indiannavy.nic.in/node/18447 (Accessed April 21, 2020).
23. "Flood Relief Operations in Sri Lanka by Indian Navy", *Indian Navy,* May 27, 2017 at https://www.indiannavy.nic.in/node/17030 (Accessed April 21, 2020).
24. "HADR Assistance by 1st Training Squadron to Indonesia", *Indian Navy,* October 2, 2018 at https://www.indiannavy.nic.in/node/20925 (Accessed April 21, 2020).
25. "Indian Navy steps up anti-piracy patrol", *The Hindu,* June 2, 2019 at https://www.thehindu.com/news/national/indian-navy-deploys-p-8i-from-oman-on-anti-piracy-patrols-in-gulf-of-aden/article27406710.ece (Accessed April 21, 2020).
26. Press Information Bureau (2018), "Raksha Mantri Inaugurates Information Fusion Centre – Indian Ocean Region (IFC-IOR)", December 22, 2018 at https://pib.gov.in/newsite/PrintRelease.aspx?relid=186757 (Accessed April 21, 2020).
27. "Statement by India–General Debate, First Committee", *United Nations,* October 14, 2019 at https://www.un.org/disarmament/wp-content/uploads/2019/10/statement-by-india-gd-oct-14-19.pdf

11

Afghanistan in India's Security Calculus

Amar Sinha

Background

India's relations with Afghanistan are historical with much of the past tied to present-day Afghanistan and the areas beyond. People, ideas, cultural influences, languages and also invading armies arrived in 'Hindustan' along this route. Given this deep connection, one can discern an emotional bond between the two peoples. 'Hindustan' always held a special allure in the region beyond the Indus. The partition of India in 1947 took away the common border, but the old links were not obliterated. That loss of contiguity is lamented in both countries. Unfortunately, the parts of Jammu and Kashmir that abut Afghanistan are currently under the occupation of Pakistan.

Today India and Afghanistan are part of the same geo-political space and are members of the South Asian Association for Regional Corporation (SAARC). But in the past, large tracts of these two nations have been part of the same kingdom—at times Afghan and at times Indian. Kabul was as dear to Mughal emperor Babur as to any 'Kabulii' today. It is no surprise that as per Babur's wishes, his body is interred in Kabul in the beautiful setting of *Bagh-e-Babur*. These historical interlinkages and contiguity, created interdependence that allowed for trade, easy movement of people and educational and cultural exchanges. Till as late as 1978, the land route was open for traffic both ways and indeed Europeans and others arrived in India overland through Afghanistan. Multiple international upheavals of 1979 changed that completely. One is familiar with stories of Indians travelling to Kabul for honeymooning, and people from Kabul driving through Pakistan to India for shopping, seeking education or medical facilities. The partition, and subsequent Pakistani policy of disallowing travel and transit, affected Afghanistan in various ways and contributed to its heightened sense of being landlocked. Sitting astride the crossroads of empires and civilisations, it always used to be a 'roundabout' and not a *cul-de sac* as its current President often recalls.

The people who lived in the Federally Administered Tribal Area (FATA), more popularly known as the Af-Pak region, straddling the Durand Line, which had separated the British area of influence from that of Afghanistan, were prescient (even today many call themselves Afghans- not to be confused with current nationality). Their leader, Khan Abdul Ghaffar Khan, a close associate of Mahatma Gandhi, had foreseen the fate that awaited them post-partition and hence opposed the British plans vehemently. He was a bitter man when the partition did happen, and ruefully told Gandhi that 'you have thrown us to the wolves'. Similarly, the dispensation in Kabul was upset that the British were leaving without any clarity on the Durand Line which Pakistan, as an inheritor state, claimed as its international boundary.

This was immediately repudiated by Afghanistan which claimed the traditional Pashtun lands, and also Baluchistan, as part of its own historical territory. In fact, such was the anger in Kabul that Afghanistan became the only country to vote against Pakistan joining the United Nations (UN). Thus, the seeds of mutual distrust and poor interstate relations were sown right in 1947. This critical piece of history is often overlooked by current analysts who muster up various factors, of more recent vintage, to explain what is happening in the Af-Pak region.

The situation that Afghanistan faces today arises from a number of historical and perhaps psychological causes, and a deep distrust and mind-set solidified over decades. First, Afghanistan has a long history of existing as an independent nation—it came into being 200 years before India or Pakistan emerged as nation-states. Afghans trace the origin of their nation back to 1747 when the Durrani empire was set up by Ahmed Shah Abdali. This has filled in them a deep sense of history and nationhood. Quite naturally, they deeply resent a relatively new country like Pakistan, meddling in their affairs, to the extent of controlling their fate. Then there is a long history of conflict with the adjoining region of Punjab which in the current context has been exacerbated by the actions of the Punjabi-dominated Pakistani military. Earlier bitterness has found contemporary justifications. Pakistan's continuing support to the Taliban and other terror outfits fighting in Afghanistan is deeply resented. The Pakistan military's policies have remained a thorn in the side of the both India and Afghanistan. The region is still paying for the partition, and this one decision of the British in 1947 has turned the region into a 'dangerous neighbourhood'.

It is in this context that the Afghans feel drawn to India—both as its historical neighbour and a reliable partner during the decades that Afghanistan has been in conflict, and before. India's principled policies of support to the central government in Kabul, not only now, but throughout its history, except for the brief interregnum when the Pakistan-backed Taliban took over Kabul between 1996 and 2001, is well recognised and appreciated.

Much has been written about the Soviet intervention in Afghanistan, the ensuing war and the eventual withdrawal of the USSR and collapse of the communist regime in Kabul. In fact, India at that point had found itself stranded on the wrong side of Afghan public opinion due to its very special relations with the Soviets following the Friendship Treaty and events of 1971. Even though not entirely accurate, Afghans still recall that India, as a leader of the nonaligned world, did not stand up for Afghan sovereignty, when their nation was 'invaded and occupied' by the USSR.

Factors Defining India and Afghanistan Relations

The turnaround that has been witnessed in India-Afghanistan relations, particularly after the US overthrowing the Taliban regime post-9/11, can only be called breathtaking. Afghanistan has truly emerged from the chaos of the fratricidal civil war, the dark period of the Taliban, to devote itself to rebuilding the country brick by brick: its devastated or non-existent infrastructure, a political framework based on an Islamic but modern constitution, requisite institutions and mechanisms for delivery of services, and apparatus for local governance. It has successfully created the sinews required to run and manage a modern nation state. All this has happened despite a deadly enemy, emboldened by the support and succour it has received from Pakistan, unleashing untold death and destruction. The fact that India has been a partner in all the positive changes one sees in Afghanistan is a matter of great satisfaction. Afghanistan has received generous support from the international community.

Since 2001, India has lent strong political support and developmental assistance to the Kabul government and has quietly gone about reconstruction of this war-devastated country. Afghans have noted that India does not play partisan or ethnic politics in Afghanistan nor does it indulge in what can be termed 'choosing the winners'. That has been a unique USP of India—committed, solidly behind Kabul, but not interfering.

India stood by her friends when it brought to safety the family of former President Mohammed Najibullah. It was unfortunate that Najibullah could not be extricated in good time, due to infighting in Afghanistan, and met a tragic end at the hands of the Taliban.

The Modi Regime

While Indian policies towards Afghanistan have been consistent, the arrival of Prime Minister Narendra Modi gave this relationship a new impetus. A new energy was injected in all that India did. All pending projects and requests were processed faster and executed efficiently. The leadership in India kept Afghanistan under regular review and that had an electrifying effect. Projects that had languished for years were pursued with a sense of purpose, and within two years of the Modi Government taking over, he inaugurated both the iconic Salma Dam (now known as India Afghanistan Friendship Dam) as well as the Afghan parliament building constructed by India. Both these projects, with immense utilitarian as well as symbolic importance, had been going on for nearly 10 years with no end in sight. But fixing responsibility and pinning accountability on the implementing agencies, and reviews at the highest level had the desired effect. In 2014, the long talked about Chabahar port project was also brought to the top of the agenda, and within two years India had MOUs and Agreements with Iran. This provides Afghanistan an alternative route to the sea, while it is critical for India's access to Afghanistan and Central Asia. This new sense of purpose was not lost on the Afghans.

Modi's personal standing and popularity in Afghanistan was very high, and his government's robust response to Pakistan and laser-like focus on terrorism emanating from Pakistan was music to Afghan ears. In Modi, the Afghans discovered a champion for their own cause—wounded as they were from the unrelenting assault from Pak-based terror groups. The issue of terror found centre space in all statements and declarations that India put its seal on—bilateral, regional or multilateral. The Indian focus on the Pakistani role in sponsoring cross-border terror ended up highlighting its negative role in Afghanistan that had gone unchallenged for years.

The earlier hesitation on actively supporting Afghanistan's war efforts was shed, and India emerged as one of the biggest training partner for Afghan security forces. While it was NATO's responsibility to train and equip Afghan forces specialised training was made available along with some equipment to fill the gaps. The set of combat helicopters gifted from India's active inventory was a game-changer for the Afghan forces that needed air support and aerial mobility. These were momentous decisions, and perhaps, for the first time, Afghans felt that their strategic partnership with India was actually working. The scholarship programme was expanded and all 1000 slots fully utilised. Children of Afghan National Security Forces (ANSF) martyrs were covered under a new scholarship programme. This was another first, where Indian scholarship went to support school education. Great emphasis was put on skill development and other civilian training and new levels of higher education in India were opened up for Afghan students. India also committed to construct housing for Afghan refugees and internally displaced people (IDPs). Thus, the Modi era in some way can be described as 'walk the talk' when it came to her relationship with Afghanistan..

When India joined the United Nations Security Council (UNSC) as a non-permanent member it needs to be recalled that it was due to Afghanistan withdrawing its candidature in favour of India. This was Afghanistan leadership's way of conveying their thanks, confident as they were that India would speak for them as well.

India's Strategy in Afghanistan

Afghanistan figures high in India's security matrix. It is derived from India's past experience of the Taliban regime when Afghanistan had become a playground for terror groups and mercenaries and jehadists from around the world looking for a cause. The so called 'jehad' against the Soviets incubated by Pakistan soon got support of several actors, and had become a magnet for radicals and terrorists. The loss of Bangladesh was a trauma that Pakistan found difficult to come to terms with and in this context the withdrawal of the USSR in 1989 encouraged Pakistan to seek 'strategic depth' across the Durand Line, which in their reckoning could only be achieved through a pliable government in Kabul. Pakistan wanted a dispensation in Kabul that was willing to turn a blind eye to the relocation of the India focussed terror groups on to its territory. Pakistan sought deniability for its policy of support to terrorist outfits, as it helped change the narrative on Jammu and Kashmir – from a bilateral territorial dispute to a religious one which was firing up the religiously motivated groups. There ecosystem for such an enterprise already had already been created in Afghanistan with global terrorist finding hospitality under the Taliban regime. In this mix Pakistan found it easy to relocate the groups it had nurtured for use against India.

All nationalist forces opposed to the Taliban, were branded as the 'northern alliance' and a narrative of inter-ethnic civil war was peddled. While it is true that the Taliban was largely a Pashtun force, those opposed to it also had a mix of all ethnic groups. Over the years Taliban has worked to shed this limiting ethnic labelling and has made efforts at diversifying its support base, recruiting members from different backgrounds, and recently, a minority Shia was appointed as one of its shadow provincial governor. Despite this, the Taliban find it difficult to live down its past – of harsh imposition of extreme and radical interpretation of Islam, its discriminatory treatment of ethnic minorities and women, or its two decades long bloody campaign. While denied by the Taliban recent past has seen a number of high profile attacks specifically targeting the minority Shia community.

Afghanistan society is incredibly diverse and good governance requires embracing its diversity and following a policy of accommodation and tolerance. While the geography and sociology of Afghanistan suggests a loose federal structure of governance, it also needs a strong and inclusive central authority as a rallying point, which retains the capability to exercise control over its entire territory. This reality has guided India's support to a strong and independent Afghan government. Conversely, a volatile Afghanistan, or one which has a weak and ineffective government, should be of great concern to India and other neighbours.

It is not clear that Taliban has changed sufficiently, despite recent statements, to provide any level of comfort to the global community. It is pertinent to remember that large numbers of regional terrorists were pushed out of Pakistan in 2014-2015 when the Pakistan military conducted its operation 'zarb-e-azb' in its FATA region. Elements of Al-Qa'ida (AQ), Tehrik-i-Taliban Pakistan (TTP) besides, Uzbeks, Chechens and Uighurs militants have found shelter in different areas under Taliban control. Some of them have also joined the newly formed Islamic State Khorasan Province (ISKP) or ISIS-K which is acting as a new magnet which is drawing volunteers from several nations, including a few from India. While the Taliban is ideologically opposed to ISIS-K, it also makes operational accommodation due to the structure and patronage system that operates for these terror outfits. The chief of AQ in any case has pledged allegiance to Taliban's amir ul momineen, while the Haqqani network, described as 'veritable arm of the ISI' is now in leadership position in the Taliban. Despite the serious blowback suffered by Pakistani society from its military's terrorist-friendly policies the Pakistan 'deep state' does not seem convinced of the need for a course correction.

The recent reports to the UNSC, as also of the US Government, pinpoint Pakistan's continuing support to the Taliban and other terror groups, and the Taliban's continuing dalliance with the AQ despite its commitments in the agreement of Feb 29, 2020 with the US. Anyway, the different terror groups are so interdependent and interlinked that it is difficult to identify and isolate them based on any flag or ideology. This situation calls for alertness on part of India.

US Efforts in Afghanistan and Future Scenarios

The US desire to have lasting peace and stability in Afghanistan is an objective that is totally shared by India and reflects the overwhelming Afghan public opinion and national aspiration after nearly four decades of war and violence. The majority of the Afghan population, which is young and aspirational, unfortunately has seen nothing but war. This post 9/11 generation is increasingly educated, aware and well connected with rest of the world and seeks normalcy. The US-Taliban talks spread over 18 months created a road map for US and NATO troop withdrawal while the Taliban committed to sever its links with AQ and other terror groups, and engage in intra Afghan negotiations that would lead to peace and cessation of violence that Afghanistan has been waiting for. Departure of all foreign troops from Afghan soil has been a consistent Taliban demand and a starting point for any move towards reconciliation. US has met the key demands of the Taliban. Taliban has to now hold up its end of the Agreement. The withdrawal issue, however, could have been handled differently since the USA has a Strategic Partnership Agreement, and also signed a Bilateral Security Agreement (BSA) in 2014 with the Kabul government. The BSA not only determines the nature and scope of their partnership but also governs the conditions under which the USA troops can remain in Afghanistan. Thus, a notice to the Afghan government would have been adequate for an orderly withdrawal. However, an agreement with Taliban, US's main adversary, was needed more for optics, if the USA was not to be accused of leaving the job half done. Perhaps it was also needed to deny the Taliban and its supporters bragging rights on defeating yet another super power.

The negotiations with the Taliban went on considerably longer than what the US negotiators had initially envisaged. Though the Agreement appears one sided in terms of concessions granted to the Taliban, it has opened the door for intra-Afghan negotiations and presents a historic opportunity for a breakthrough. However, increasingly it appears the real intention of the Taliban is not to work towards peace and reconciliation, but to replace the Islamic Republic of Afghanistan by its Islamic Emirates version 2.0. The intra-Afghan talk that was to commence on 10 March 2020, started only on 12 September but took another three months to just agree on the rules and procedures. In the meantime, all round violence by Taliban has been dialled up substantially. It appears that the Taliban wishes to maximise its gains before entering into any meaningful dialogue hence they have kept up pressure on Afghan military and provincial capitals. Now with the extended deadline for troop withdrawal approaching there is little incentive left for the Taliban to engage in any serious negotiations, It was not the first time US tried for a negotiated settlement. The Doha office started in 2014 under President Barack Obama, with a core of 5 or 6 ex-Guantanamo bay prisoners though that initiative was quickly aborted after vociferous protest from the Afghan government, which objected to the Taliban attempts to give their Doha political office the trappings of the seat of a government in exile. It would be recalled that the Taliban was also engaged in a quadrilateral format in 2015 (Pakistan, China, USA and Afghanistan) but that process too got derailed after the first round, when the news that Mullah Omar, founder-leader of the movement, being dead for nearly three years became public. This had exposed the duplicity of the Taliban, as well as the Pakistani agency, for keeping a fiction alive and also issuing periodic messages from a deceased Amir! While the US desire to bring their longest war to an end is understandable, it the manner in which this is sought to be implemented has divided opinions even within the USA. The US-Taliban Agreement has bestowed an element of legitimacy on the Taliban while undermining the democratically elected government of Afghanistan. The Afghan desire for ceasefire and peace has been deprioritised with no obligation imposed on the Taliban, nor a clear or enforceable timeline set for the intra Afghan talks. Cessation of violence has been left to be an outcome of the negotiations thus forcing the Afghan government to negotiate with a gun pointed to its head while 5000 prisoners have been released unconditionally. This sequencing in effect has built in a certain tolerance for continuing Taliban attacks against Afghan civilian and military targets. There is persistent danger of public opinion favouring accommodation changing, if the Taliban atrocities continue. Besides, it also leaves room for 'spoilers' uncomfortable with peace returning to Afghanistan. The process can be easily derailed by using non-Taliban terror groups in Afghan theatre. In such a situation Afghanistan spiralling into a fresh cycle of violence cannot be ruled out. Quo Vadis?

Afghans do not believe that Taliban will take over Kabul militarily since despite the claims made by the Taliban it has not succeeded in urban areas and are in a stalemate. The ANSF capabilities are well known and it has been conducting majority of the operations on its own since 2014. The apprehensions revolve around the long term commitment of the USA to Afghanistan after its exit. That would be a *déjà vu* of sorts –a replay of the developments post-Soviet withdrawal. By now it is also clear that important neighbours of Afghanistan will not countenance Taliban having a monopoly on power in Afghanistan. It is hoped history does not replay itself after 30 years since the war has stymied Afghanistan's economic potential. Economic regeneration needs extended periods of peace that has been elusive. Domestic resources, while growing, have fallen short of the requirements making Afghanistan dependent on external assistance. However, the Kabul government under President Ashraf Ghani has done different financial modelling to see how the costs of war could be brought down to South Asian levels. It is unlikely that regional countries, however rich they may be, will step in to fill the void the USA and NATO will leave behind. The expectation that a resource-rich China would step in to fill the breach is a distant possibility at best. China is too closely aligned to the Pakistani position to take an independent line on Afghanistan, and their concern as of now is unidimensional—neutralising the Uighurs.

Thus, for now, the future of Afghanistan remains uncertain, and to a very large extent it would depend on what pressures are brought on the Taliban to forsake violence and reintegrate. First and foremost, their access to their sanctuaries and safe havens will have to be shut down for them to come to the negotiating table.

(The views expressed by the author were before the fall of Afghanistan to the Taliban forces)

12

De-Securitisation and National Security: Reflections on India's Policy towards Pakistan

T.C.A. Raghavan

Juxtaposing national interest and national security in the case of Pakistan does not require lengthy explanations. For a very long period of time, the dominant ethos and narrative in Pakistan has been that national interest is nothing else but national security. Such a view emerged and cemented itself largely as a consequence of Pakistan's long experience of military-dominated governance with relatively brief periods when the political class had a major role in the country's polity. "Pakistan as a Fortress" illustrates this and it has meant obviously a worldview and a mindset that is highly and excessively securitized, prone to thinking in terms of zero sum games, in which the geopolitical easily outweighs the geo economic and, finally, there is the inability to disaggregate the tactical from the strategic and the long term.

This failure to disaggregate national security from national interests has led to Pakistan developing a flawed narrative in dealing with the central questions which many countries in adverse geopolitical environments inevitably face.

Political wisdom lies in seeing national interest as the conglomeration of many factors—economic development, social cohesion, equitable growth, internal security, etc. National security is obviously one among these factors but not the only one. In Pakistan, the failure to see this somewhat obvious point explains most of its past and current dilemmas.

Pakistan's Afghanistan policy illustrates both this failure and also how excessive securitisation germinates failure. From the 1980s onwards, when Pakistan emerged as a frontline state in the US-led effort against the Soviets in Afghanistan, it had numerous positives going for it insofar as many Afghans were concerned. It gave, for instance, refuge to large numbers of displaced persons at great cost to itself. It is useful to recall that, although the two situations are vastly different, in per capita terms the burden on Pakistan from Afghan refugees has been more and for a much longer period than what India faced during the Bangladesh crisis and the refugee influx. Through the 1990s and thereafter Pakistan's cities—Quetta, Peshawar and increasingly Karachi—were important centres for Afghans seeking safe residence, medical treatment, education and also for business. Afghanistan's dependence on Pakistan for many items of mass consumption is considerable. Land-locked Afghanistan's—especially the eastern and southern parts—dependence on Pakistani ports as an inlet and outlet is another dimension of the interface between the two countries that demonstrates how heavily it is weighted in favour of Pakistan.

These factors and advantages, and this list can be extended a great deal, all should have led Pakistan to invest in and develop a well-rounded relationship with Afghanistan. Such a relationship would have enabled a contextualisation of the serious differences neighbouring countries often have, such as the Durand Line issue for Pakistan and Afghanistan, and by so doing have prevented relations between the two from deteriorating.

What we have instead seen of Pakistan policy towards Afghanistan since the 1990s has been the opposite. Instead of reaping huge public goodwill from its hosting of Afghanistan refugees, it found itself against a mounting wave of public revision and dislike in Afghanistan on account of intervention in its internal affairs and efforts to keep the situation there from stabilising. Much of this can be traced to the use of armed proxies and insurgent groups to influence internal developments in Afghanistan, i.e., using Afghanistan's fault lines to incubate instability as a means to expand Pakistan's influence and leverage. Whether driven by flawed theories of strategic depth or by deep-rooted insecurities about Afghan non-acceptance of the Durand Line as a border, over the past three decades Pakistan's Afghan policy has exposed its fundamental flaws by its major failures.

This demonstrates the classic failure arising out of a security-driven approach towards a neighbour. The policy failed most significantly in terms of its domestic consequences for Pakistan. The first decade and a half of this century saw the country tottering on the brink of an internal security melt down largely on account of the security backlash from the proxies it had nurtured to leverage the situation in Afghanistan. Even more destabilising was the wider ecosystem of religious radicalism that sustained these proxies. This ecosystem expanded within Pakistan, radicalised other sections of society, encouraged sectarianism and in general contributed even further to the internal security erosion within. If these internal consequences were devastating for Pakistan, the gains from this, if any, in Afghanistan are fragmentary and elusive especially when compared to the numerous advantages Pakistan has with regard to its land-locked neighbour. To summarise a well-known story, by the end of the first decade of this century, Pakistan found its influence in Afghanistan tethered to the single pole of the Taliban, its image in Afghanistan deeply tarnished, perhaps irreparably, and finally internally within Pakistan, a country at war with itself.

There is of course the perspective that the sands are shifting once again and the re-ordering of Afghanistan's political architecture to the advantage of the Taliban will be a vindication of Pakistan's policy approach. This view again is premised largely on a tactical approach and overlooks the longer term issues that bedevil Pakistan's policy—poor image in Afghanistan, risks of blowback into Pakistan of further conflicts in Afghanistan, etc. But the seductions of a securitized approach are such that these factors are rarely considered in the actual framing of policy, whether external or domestic. In the words of a former Pakistan Foreign Secretary:[1]

> *"[The] long periods of military rule and influence induced a security orientation in state thinking, creating a justification for high expenditures to maintain military preparedness against perceived threats. Security became the central strategic concern. This view was so well entrenched that, following the nuclear tests and overt establishment of deterrence and strategic balance with India, the suggestion to divert resources from defence immediately drew a counter-argument that conventional balance was also necessary in order to keep the nuclear threshold high. The influence of the military elite on the polarized and often unstable politics did not allow civilian political leaders to shift the governance paradigm from its emphasis on security to one that addressed the complex issues of welfare, development, and political cohesion."*

Many of the issues that exist in Pakistan's polity with respect to Afghanistan in terms of an excessive securitisation can be found in its approach to India also, especially in terms of using armed proxies and terrorism as an instrument of state policy in Jammu & Kashmir and elsewhere. The differences, however, are also important and significant emerging largely from the much larger space that India occupies in Pakistan's mental landscape as also the structurally rooted revisionism regarding Kashmir. Nevertheless, it is useful to keep Pakistan's security-driven mindset as a backdrop when reviewing recent developments in India and Pakistan relations.

An 'engagement-disengagement' binary has characterised India and Pakistan relations for the past quarter century. In this period, India has had six prime ministers, five different governments and seven general elections. Virtually every part of the political spectrum of the country has, at some point of time in this period, either formed the government or been in it as part of a coalition or a supporter. In the same period in Pakistan there have been 10 prime ministers and five general elections. In between 1999 and 2008 there was a near decade long period of military rule. Again, as in the case of India, over this quarter century virtually the entire political spectrum of Pakistan has been associated with government, in one form or the other.

The engagement-disengagement binary has very evidently a structural basis. It is also a fact that this binary has intensified in both directions over time. The greater the intensity of engagement, equally significant and fraught has been the disengagement that followed. The Lahore Bus Initiative was followed by Kargil, the Agra Summit followed by the attack on India's Parliament, the CBM/structured dialogue process of 2004-2008 was severely undermined by the Mumbai terrorist attack of November 2008 and the Pathankot attack in January 2016 followed the Prime Minister's visit to Lahore a few days earlier. There are other instances also.

It is also interesting that new initiatives with respect to engagement, or for that matter disengagement, have not been a consequence of political change in terms of a new government reversing polices of its predecessor. Engagement, disengagement and engagement again has characterised policies of the same government. The NDA under Prime Minister Atal Bihari Vajpayee from 1998 to 2004 went from engagement to disengagement to engagement to disengagement and ended its tenure on a high note of engagement. This diplomacy encapsulated a tumultuous history through the Lahore Bus Initiative, Kargil, the hijacking of IC 814, the Agra Summit, the terrorist attack on our Parliament, Operation Parakaram and the Islamabad Summit. UPA-I disengaged following the Mumbai serial blasts of July 2006 but reversed that course by instituting the Joint Anti Terrorism Mechanism. Such examples can be cited up to the recent past, e.g., the opening of the Kartarpur Corridor in the midst of a high period of India–Pakistan tensions.

During this period, the central issue of terrorism has been the factor responsible for placing the greatest strain on India and Pakistan relations and diplomacy. This history is well known and need not be recapitulated. In the period after the Pathankot airbase terrorist attack (January, 2016) India and Pakistan relations moved into a new phase. The principal milestones of the process follow from the major terrorist attacks on Indian security forces in Uri (September 2016) and Pulwama (February 2019). The feature that emerged thereafter was that kinetic responses would acquire a strategic dimension in terms of signalling both to Pakistan and to domestic public opinion the postures of the Government of India with regard to the threat of terrorist attacks from Pakistan.

This kinetic phase obvious marks significant changes from the earlier Indian responses to terrorist attacks. This is not necessarily to detract from the substance of earlier responses such as Operation Parakaram after the attack on Parliament or mobilising intellectual pressure post the 26/11 attack on Mumbai. The point is that our postures have varied over time and also injected a healthy dose of unpredictability to our response portfolio. Yet it is also the case that kinetic responses alone cannot be the single pillar on which the edifice of a Pakistan policy can be built for India. To do so would be to embark on a course that limits and constrains our policy options to a heavily securitized approach.

The foreign policy of any country is based on a wide spectrum deriving in turn from the country's economy, cultural strength and projection, its political narratives, etc. While an adversarial relationship with Pakistan has meant that the relationship has also to be viewed by India in security terms, an entirely securitized relationship is not a desirable outcome particularly from India's point of view. Pakistan's continued use of terrorists as an instrument of state policy does require kinetic responses as was effectively demonstrated by the surgical strikes post Uri or the Balakot strike post Pulwama. Nevertheless, kinetic responses on the border cannot be the only instrument in our policy toolkit in dealing with Pakistan. In this regard we have to constantly evaluate the possibility of introducing non-security elements into the India-Pakistan agenda whenever feasible. Feasibility is, of course, important for this obviously cannot be done at random and the timing of initiatives in this direction has to be located within the overall context of bilateral relations.

Over the past seven decades there have been three principal attempts by India to de-securitise the India-Pakistan agenda apart from regular diplomatic processes to bolster people-to-people contacts and cultural exchanges. This has been attempted by introducing elements from the non-traditional security domain principally as a means of reducing the intensity of existing differences. Two of these attempts were failures; one was, relatively speaking, a greater success. The success story was in the division of the Indus system of rivers through a treaty that pragmatically ring fenced river waters sharing from all the other contestations of India and Pakistan geopolitics including Jammu and Kashmir. This ring fencing could not, however, be enlarged or deepened largely as a result of the political turn Pakistan took post-1965 and especially after 1989. The two failures were in the field of energy—represented by the Iran-Pakistan-India (IPI) gas pipeline—and economics: the prolonged suboptimal levels of trade ending finally in a logjam in 2019 which will require great skill of political initiative to undo. The reasons for the failures are obvious enough: the IPI gas pipeline proved to be a bridge too far because of the difficulties in combining India and Pakistan issues with the geopolitics of Iran. The trade initiative was also full of promise but faced the problem that the two economies are basically competitive rather than complementary and the difference in size meant that balance of trade issues acquired greater prominence than would have been otherwise. Other domains of non-traditional security—climate change, glacial melt, water availability, environmental pollution—have developed only a limited traction in the India-Pakistan context largely because these spill over into the domain of traditional geopolitics and security issues. This means a burden too heavy for the science involved to bear on its own.

De-securitisation has in fact been an implicit part of our policy approach up to this day and has existed even in the period after the surgical strikes of 2016 when a robust securitized approach has defined India's approach to Pakistan to a great extent. Despite a period of high tension and poor bilateral atmospherics, a significant measure in the form of the opening of the Kartarpur Saheb Corridor (November, 2019) was put in place. A step that would have been difficult to take in the best of times was taken at the near worst of times. Significant breakthroughs of this kind in the past are associated with periods of upswings in bilateral relations—the Kokraphar–Munabao Rail Link in 2006 or the Srinagar–Muzaffarabad Bus Service in 2005; for instance, both took place at a time when India and Pakistan relations were looking better than they had for decades, perhaps ever, and constructive engagement was at a high. The fact that a long-standing demand, considered and not found possible to implement many times earlier, of the Sikh community would be agreed to and implemented by both governments at a time of very high tension when their relations were minimal is thus both unusual and significant.

Similarly in the wake of the COVID-19 pandemic, the convening of a SAARC leaders meet both underscored the narrative value of regional cooperation as also in effacing the global pandemic and other disputes put aside. The challenge for our foreign policy and diplomacy with adversarial neighbours in the future will be to combine a securitized approach with a de-securitisation agenda and seeking to expand the profile of de-securitisation in India's overall policy profile. That this is not easy goes without saying. Nevertheless in the pursuit of national interest any other approach in the medium and long term risks being sub optimal.

NOTES

1. Riaz Mohammad Khan, Afghanistan and Pakistan: Conflict, Extremism and Resistance to Modernity, Oxford University Press, Karachi, 2011, p. 315.

13

India-China Confidence Building Measures

S.L. Narashimhan

Introduction

India and China are two big neighbours with a combined population of over 2.82 billion. Both are ancient civilisations having experienced princely kingdoms and feudal systems. Buddhism, which emanated from India, found resonance in China. Even today, China is home to 244,130,000 Buddhists who make up 18.2 per cent of its population.[1] While India achieved its independence from British colonial rule after decades of struggle for freedom, in August 1947; China went through a civil war before the communist leader, Mao Zedong, declared the creation of the People's Republic of China (PRC) in October 1949. Seven decades of relationship between India and China has seen fluctuating fortunes, including war. The former Premier of China, Wen Jiabao, at a meeting with the visiting Defence Minister George Fernandes in 2003, mentioned that 99.9 per cent of the time both the countries have had good relations. Trust and goodwill defined the period between 1949 and 1957 with the two countries agreeing in 1954 on *Panchsheel*, the five principles of coexistence.

From a high in 1954, the relationship, in a span of five years, became irreconcilable by the events in Tibet and the unsettled borders in the Himalayas. With talks between Jawaharlal Nehru and Zhou Enlai having failed in 1960, the two countries were staring down the barrel. The India-China war of 1962 that lasted about a month had shaken India's belief of never being attacked by China. The war brought in a hiatus in the bilateral relationship for 15 years. It was only when External Affairs Minister Y.B. Chavan announced in Parliament in April 1976 that India was sending an ambassador (K.R. Narayanan) to Peking that the relationship started thawing again.[2] But before that, India had gone nuclear in 1974 and, not surprisingly, it was not received well in China even though China had conducted its nuclear test 10 years earlier.[3] With the re-establishment of diplomatic relations at the ambassadorial level, there was an effort to resolve the boundary issue between both the countries. However, these talks did not proceed well.

In 1988, at the invitation of Premier Li Peng, Prime Minister Rajiv Gandhi visited China (the last such visit by an Indian prime minister was in 1954 when Nehru had met Mao). This marked an important phase of India-China relations; an earnest effort commenced to improve the bilateral relationship and to resolve the intractable boundary issues. During the period 1993–2013, a number of agreements were signed. In the late 1990s, dehyphenation of China-India and China-Pakistan relations took place. Around the time, it was also decided to broaden the bilateral relations to other areas of mutual interest like economy and trade, people-to-people contacts and delink them from the boundary issue. The progress on the boundary talks was, however, not much to write home about. It prompted a setting up of a Special Representatives Mechanism during Prime Minister Vajpayee's visit to China in 2003.[4] It is against this background that we need to look at Confidence Building Measures between India and China. This has become critically important due to the prevailing situation along the Line of Actual Control (LAC). An effort is made in this chapter to look at the Confidence Building Measures that can be adopted to improve the relationship between India and China.

However, an important caveat is necessary at this stage. China is a big neighbour and cannot be wished away. The actions of China in the past several months along the LAC have resulted in strained relations. Unless the *status quo ante*—as existing before China mobilised its troops in 2020—is achieved, it will be difficult to keep the bilateral relations on an even keel. Unlike in the past when the boundary-related incidents were kept separate from the other parts of the relationship, this time such a separation is not possible.[5] Therefore, it is in the interest of maintaining peace and tranquillity along the LAC that China should carry out the disengagement, as agreed upon, both in letter and spirit. The damage that has been done to the relationship will take time, considerable effort and a lot of resources to bring it back to normal.

Convergences and Divergences

In order to understand what all has been done and how to improve India-China relations, it is imperative to look at the divergences and convergences in the bilateral relationship.

Divergences

The first and foremost divergence between India and China is the territorial boundary, commonly referred to as the 'boundary question'. The boundary issue is complex and needs careful handling particularly when the views differ radically between the two countries. The other question is China's relationship with Pakistan which acts as an impediment to the progress of relations between India and China.[6] Despite India trying to keep the China-Pakistan nexus away from its overall relationship with China, the latter's support to Pakistan in the UN on terrorism and Kashmir has not been helpful. China has equally not been comfortable with the Tibetan government and His Holiness the Dalai Lama in exile in India. China considers the Dalai Lama a political figure harbouring intentions of splitting Tibet from China.[7] In 2004, Booz Allen Hamilton brought out a study that said China is weaving a string of pearls around India by increasing its influence in India's neighbourhood.[8] It cannot be denied that China's growing influence in the neighbourhood has led to competition and rivalry between India. Interestingly, India follows a policy of 'neighbourhood first'[9] and China follows the policy of 'friendly neighbourhood'.[10] This goes to show that both the countries have neighbourhood as a foreign policy priority. The economies of China and India have grown rapidly and it is widely felt that these two 'emerging giants' will impact and transform the global economy in significant ways. With economic growth for both the countries projected to increase in the coming decade, the demand for energy, minerals and access to markets would also grow. Competition for natural resources will be a prominent feature of their interaction. China has already established a base in Djibouti on the Horn of Africa and Gwadar, a town in Pakistan's Balochistan province, may become a strategically important site for its People's Liberation Army Navy. China is one of the biggest investors in various infrastructure projects in Sri Lanka including financing the strategic southern port of Hambantota. Likewise, China has access to the Chittagong and Mangla seaports in Bangladesh and has formed a new economic partnership, as part of the One Belt, One Road Initiative (OBOR), with Myanmar to develop its deep-sea ports and other multi-million projects. The Kyaukpyu port in the Bay of Bengal when developed will not be far from India's submarine base in Vishakapatnam.

There also seems to be competition in providing disaster relief. Due to its geographical location and its capability to be a first responder, India was quick in providing relief to the countries during the tsunami in 2004, in the Maldives water crisis in 2014 and during the earthquake that Nepal suffered in 2015. However, in all these disaster-related and humanitarian crises China, in a bid for regional influence, tried to reach out to the stricken countries by providing relief. It rushed in bottled water to Maldives and also relief material to Nepal soon after India had responded to the crisis. While China insists on its 'One China' policy, it desists from supporting the 'One India' policy. China has also not been supportive of India in the latter's quest to get a Permanent Membership in the UN Security Council. China is one of the very few countries that oppose India's entry into the Nuclear Suppliers Group (NSG) citing Pakistan's non-admission into this exclusive group.[11] Since decisions in the NSG are taken on the basis of consensus, an objection raised by even one country acts as a veto.

China is known to do business with controversial regimes while

India weighs its foreign policy on ideas of exceptionalism and moral responsibilities. This is borne out by the fact that many of the countries with whom China has signed MoUs on the OBOR are either financially unstable or have weak governing systems. China being an upper riparian has not signed a water-sharing agreement with any of its co-riparian countries. The issue of China constructing dams on the up-reaches of the Yarlung Tsangpo (Brahmaputra) river and periodic information on its intention to divert the Tsangpo towards its high water demand areas in the north gets sufficiently highlighted in India.[12] Despite the fact that China has said that the dams are run-of-the-river and no physical evidence is seen, as yet for the purported diversion of the river waters, this has created enormous suspicion and a trust-deficit with India. The trade balance with China is another cause of concern for India. Trade deficit for India was USD 48.66 billion in 2019-20. Such deficit is not sustainable and creates doubts in the minds of the people about the intention of China towards a fair trade with India. In a poll that was held in 2013, 83 per cent of Indians consider China as a threat.[13] The OBOR initiative started by China in September 2013 included the China-Pakistan Economic Corridor (CPEC) that runs through India's territory of Gilgit-Baltistan. Because of this and a few other reasons like lack of transparency and contracts going mainly to Chinese companies led to India not supporting or joining this initiative. This has been a bone of contention between India and China.

The Indo-Pacific concept that was enunciated by Japan and is being pursued by the USA has created suspicion in the minds of the Chinese. Prime Minister Modi's talk in the Shangri La Dialogue in 2018[14] set the suspicion somewhat to rest. QUAD which started in 2007 and was discontinued soon thereafter was revived in 2017. This is also perceived by China to be an anti-China effort by the QUAD countries. Regional Comprehensive Economic Partnership (RCEP) is yet another divergence in India-China relations. Negotiations for RCEP which started in 2014 did not take into account India's concerns about the partnership not being comprehensive. It did not include all the aspects of the economy like trading in goods, services and movement of professionals. China and other countries have decided to go ahead with the RCEP without India being part of it.

Convergences

Both India and China support globalisation that helps their economies to grow. They have also joined hands in creating the Asian Infrastructure Investment Bank (AIIB) and the New Development Bank also known as the BRICS Bank. These two institutions function similarly as the institutions of the Bretton Woods System like the IMF and the World Bank. The AIIB is functioning efficiently and seems to be more popular than the Asian Development Bank.[15] Both the countries have also been supportive of each other on Climate Change. Though they function differently, India and China hold similar views on anti-piracy operations. China has been consistent in deploying its naval assets to fight piracy off the coast of Somalia in the Gulf of Aden. Similarly, India also has been deploying ships for anti-piracy operations though not under the West-led task force. On issues of energy cooperation, India and China have been competing for obtaining exploratory rights and in some cases have also been functioning jointly. There has been a dialogue mechanism between both the countries on counter-terrorism since 2002. In the Shanghai Cooperation Organisation, both India and China are members. As part of military diplomacy, Indian and Chinese officers have been doing courses in each other's military institutions.

Confidence Building Measures

Many view India and China as competing and not collaborating. This is not entirely true. Culture, education, agriculture and food, counter-terrorism and space are areas where collaboration is high between the two countries. In tourism, there has been an annual dialogue that has been going on since 2002. The India-China Youth Exchange Programme has been going on since 2006-07. In the last exchange visit in 2018, a 200-member Indian youth delegation comprising students, researchers and young achievers went visiting various Chinese cities to experience the many facets of Chinese culture, society and politics.

A number of Confidence Building Measures have also been initiated to build trust amongst the Indian Armed Forces and the Chinese People's Liberation Army (PLA). Border personnel meetings at regular intervals and on special occasions like national days and other celebrations are being conducted. Friendly sports matches and exercises between troops on the border have also been conducted. Exercise 'Hand-in-Hand' that started in 2007 has been going on intermittently. These defence cooperation measures, however, have taken a back seat due to the escalation of tensions along the LAC in eastern Ladakh in 2020.

Recent Efforts

Since 2014, with the change in government in India, efforts to improve bilateral relations with China have been a priority. The Indian polity, for the first time since 1989, witnessed a clear mandate thus providing for a strong and stable government under Prime Minister Narendra Modi. Likewise, Xi Jinping, who rose to power in 2013, and was re-elected in 2018, is seen to have unprecedented power and as probably the most powerful Chinese leader since Mao. Xi, sensing the significance of a changed polity in India, visited the country in 2014. Both the leaders evinced keen interest in resolving issues that impede bilateral relations. Subsequently, Modi's visit to China in 2015 was an equally important one paving the way for wide-ranging cooperation. In the two-way visits (Xi coming to India and Modi going to China) the economic context was made explicit. Cooperation in railways, aerospace, mining, marine science, quality control, education, disaster relief, climate change, polar science and personnel exchanges were agreed upon. A state and provincial leaders forum was inaugurated by both the leaders.[16]

In 2016, an exhibition on the Gupta period was held in China. In the field of education, eight Chinese students are granted scholarships to study Hindi. Twenty-two native Chinese have been teaching the Chinese language in Kendriya Vidyalayas in India. Approximately 23,000 Indian students are studying in China and 2,000 Chinese students are studying in various universities and institutions in India. In the field of agriculture, India exports cotton, castor oil and frozen fish. Basmati rice, meat and fish form an important part of the bilateral trade. Marine exports have been increasing and it touched approximately $ 1 billion in value in the financial year 2019-20. Agreements have also been signed in the field of space collaboration for satellite remote sensing, space-based meteorology, space science, lunar and deep space exploration, satellite navigation, space components, piggy-back launching services, space education and training.

Informal Summits

Two informal summits were held between Modi and Xi Jinping. The first was held in Wuhan in April 2018. The 'Wuhan Spirit', as it is known, brought in a sense of maturity in the bilateral relationship. The LAC also became stable. Some measures such as improving people-to-people relations and jointly carrying out projects in their neighbourhood commenced. As a result, two batches of Afghan diplomats have been trained by India and China. The Wuhan Summit was followed by a second informal summit at Mamallapuram in Tamil Nadu in October 2019—the 'Chennai Connect'. The meeting laid the foundation for a trade mechanism to be discussed between the Finance Minister of India and the Chinese Vice Premier. Defence and security relations were also to be upgraded with the defence ministers of the two countries taking the proposal forward. Cooperation in the World Trade Organization and Climate Change were also discussed. However, actions of the Chinese PLA in May 2020 onwards along the LAC in eastern Ladakh and in Sikkim have resulted in almost nullifying the decisions arrived at in both the informal summits as well as the agreements and protocols signed between 1993 and 2013.

China's view of India

In order to develop further Confidence Building Measures, it is important to understand how China views India. China is apprehensive about India's major power relationships, particularly India's equations with the USA, Japan and Australia. However, there is also the realisation that India follows a foreign policy of strategic autonomy which implies that India will take decisions based simply on its interests. China appreciates the professional capability of India's military but has doubts about the capability of weapon platforms and India's defence industry. It feels that Indian soldiers are burdened with obsolete weapon systems and rely on imports for their requirements. On the other hand, China has a positive view of India's culture,

Information Technology, space capabilities, etc., but has a poor view of the standard of 4G and railway safety in India. On the economy front, China has a somewhat mixed perception with some positives but largely negatives.

Suggested Measures to Build Confidence

Not long ago, India and China used to coordinate and collaborate on global economic issues in the WTO with an objective to strengthen South-South bonding. Similarly, on climate change, the two have had more cooperation than competition and one can recall the two, along with Brazil and South Africa, having formed a bloc of four large newly-industrialised countries or the BASIC in 2009. Since then, the BASIC countries have had ministerial-level meetings 29 times confirming their commitments to multilateralism in order to address the issue of climate change and promoting low-carbon and sustainable development. Neither India nor China disagrees on voluntarily reducing carbon emissions. However, such convergences saw a decline post the 2008-2009 financial crisis. One way to rebuild the confidence is by interacting and coordinating the stance of both the countries in such multilateral organisations. Both India and China are leading consumers of energy, particularly oil. They can combine their efforts to create an oil buyers' club for getting better terms for procurement of oil. Both countries are also large economies which are in the top five of the world. There are complementarities existing between them. By leveraging these complementarities, economic cooperation can be achieved for the betterment of both the countries and their people. Military diplomacy is another area presenting enormous opportunity to build confidence and trust between the armed forces of the two countries. Examples of such activities are—enhancing the scope of the exercises being conducted between them, increasing the number and scale of sports activities between both the armed forces, increasing the number of vacancies for courses in each other's training institutions, etc. When Xi Jinping visited India in 2014 he agreed to an investment of $ 20 billion in India. If China does genuine manufacturing by utilising local manpower and raw material and increases the value addition in India to its products, it will benefit both the countries. China is strong in construction technology and manufacturing. Cooperation in these two fields will be mutually beneficial to both the countries.

To celebrate the 70th anniversary of diplomatic relations between India and China, 70 events were to be conducted. Unfortunately, with the prevailing situation on the LAC, these events, for all practical purposes, have been shelved. However, the activities identified have the potential to build friendship and mutual trust and should be pursued after normalcy returns. China's agriculture sector remains robust and is the foundation of the country's economic stability. It also is a net coarse grain importer and its import is set to increase further. For China and India, the two most populated countries, food security will be a primary objective. In the light of this, agriculture cooperation can be of great scope to improve the trade situation. India's advantage is that most of its farming products are 'non genetically modified'.

Finally, both India and China have civilisational roots and cultural values. This 'soft power' area of interaction can go a long way in building mutual trust and confidence between the state and society. Both the countries have followed a different model for population control measures. While India followed a model of awareness and education, China stressed on law by enforcing a 'one child' policy. The experience of both the countries can be exchanged to arrive at a suitable plan to achieve a demographic balance. The people of both the countries have a lot in common in behaviour and beliefs and similar kind of familial ties that they experience. There are historical similarities that link the two in a common yarn. This commonality can be worked out to build a robust relationship.

Conclusion

At present the divergences overshadow the convergences in India-China relations. If stability returns to the LAC and trust is rebuilt, then both the countries can work on overcoming the divergences and strengthening the convergences. The question is, will peace and tranquillity return?

NOTES

1. *Buddhist Countries 2020* (2020). Retrieved from World Population Review: https://worldpopulationreview.com/country-rankings/buddhist-countries
2. *India-China Bilateral Relations* (January 10, 2012). Retrieved from Ministry of External Affairs, India: file:///C:/Users/user/AppData/Local/Temp/China-January-2012.pdf
3. S. Kondapalli (July 15, 2008). China's response to Indian nuclear tests. *Strategic Analysis,* 22(3),493. Retrieved from https://www.tandfonline.com/doi/abs/10.1080/09700169808458829?journalCode=rsan20
4. *Public Diplomacy* (June 13, 2003). Retrieved from Ministry of External Affairs India: https://www.mea.gov.in/in-focusarticle.htm?7679/Declaration+on+Principles+for+Relations+and+Comprehensive+Cooperation+ Betwen+ the+Republic+ of+India+ and+the+Peoples+Republic+of+China
5. V. Varma (August, 2020). No business as usual with China till they disengage troops along LAC: Indian envoy to Russia. *Times Now News.* Retrieved from https://www.timesnownews.com/india/article/no-business-as-usual-with-china-till-they-disengagetroops-along-lac-indian-envoy-to-russia/626345
6. S. Pande (2015). Sino-Pak Strategic Relationship: Implications for India. *Scholar Warrior, Autumn,* 18-24. Retrieved from file:///C:/Users/user/AppData/Local/Temp/1942499114_SinoPakStrategicRelationship-1.pdf
7. PTI. (2019, April 5). *First Post.* Retrieved from https://www.firstpost.com/india/not-seeking-tibetsindependence-chinese-govt-wrongly-considers-me-a-splittist-says-dalai-lama-6392421.html
8. J. Drun (June 12, 2017). China's Maritime Ambitions: a Sinister String of Pearls or a Benevolent Silk Road (or Both)? *Centre for Advance China Research.* Retrieved from https://www.ccpwatch.org/singlepost/2017/12/05/China%E2%80%99s-Maritime-Ambitions-a-Sinister-String-of-Pearls-or-a-Benevolent-Silk-Road-or-Both
9. C. Xavier (Feb 15, 2020). Modi's Neighbourhood First push is being pulled down by decades of policy stagnation. *The Print.* Retrieved from https://theprint.in/opinion/modis-neighbourhood-firstpush-is-being-pulled-down-by-decades-of-policy-stagnation/365895/
10. PTI (March 12, 2018). Chinese President pitches for friendly neighbourhood policy. *Hindu Business Online.* Retrieved from https://www.thehindubusinessline.com/news/world/chinese-president-pitchesfor-friendly-neighbourhood-policy/article20681613.ece1
11. R. Chengappa (June 30, 2016). NSG: The Great Wall of Xi. *India Today.* Retrieved from https://www.indiaoday.in/magazine/the-big-story/story/20160711-nsg-membership-india-china829187-2016-06-30
12. M. Loiwal (December 13, 2017). Satellite images prove China's malafide intentions of diverting Brahmaputra water into desert. *India Today.* Retrieved from https://www.indiatoday.in/india/story/satellite-images-prove-china-malafide-intentions-of-divertingbrahmaputra-water-into-desert-1106739-2017-12-13
13. PTI (May 20, 2013). 83% Indians view China as major security threat: Survey.

Economic Times. Retrieved from politics-and-nation/83-indians-view-china-as-major-security-threatsurvey/articleshow/20155904.cms

14. Xinhua. (June 1, 2018). Shangri-la Dialogue kicks off with challenges to Asia's security taking center stage. *Xinhuanet*. Retrieved from http://www.xinhuanet.com/english/2018-06/01/c_137223798_3.htm

15. PTI (June 13, 2019). China led AIIB could overtake ADB as major financier of infra projects: Experts. *Economic Times*. Retrieved from https://economictimes.indiatimes.com/news/economy/finance/china-led-aiib-could-overtake-adb-asmajor-financier-of-infra-projectsexperts/articleshow/69773549.cms?from=mdr

16. *Media Centre* (May 15, 2015). Retrieved from Ministry of External Affairs, Govt of India: https://www.mea.gov.in/bilateraldocuments.htm?dtl/25240/Joint_Statement_between_the_India_and_China_during_Prime_Ministers_visit_to_China

14

The Modi Government's Pakistan and Kashmir Policy

Maroof Raza

On becoming the Prime Minister, Narendra Modi had inherited a Pakistan policy that had hardly led to any meaningful results. The cycle of cross-border terror attacks sponsored by Pakistan's military followed by denials by the civilian leadership, would repeatedly leave India helplessly licking its wounds. A need for change was paramount. This came following Modi's decision to dramatically alter India's responses, following the attack on a major Indian army base at Uri on the Line of Control. Consequently, surgical strikes across the Line of Control were decided. And when, Pakistan sponsored yet again terror attacks at Pulwama, India resorted to air strikes on Balakot. These two strikes on Pakistan-based terrorist camps were clearly a turning point in India-Pakistan relations.

In both the cases, Pakistan openly denied its role, but the evidences were far too clear for Pakistan to hide. There was, however, a studied silence of South Block immediately after the military responses, despite the evidence that was available about the Modi government's decision to shock and awe Pakistan. Resultantly, a large group of naysayers emerged in India questioning whether these counter-strikes had taken place inside Pakistan, or whether they were purely a propaganda of the Modi Government. Both the responses (post-Uri and post-Pulwama) were, by definition, 'surgical strikes'. Such strikes are authorized at the highest political level, the Prime Minister himself, and carried out by India's armed forces with minimum collateral damage. Most importantly, these strikes shattered the myth of Pakistan's nuclear umbrella, which its establishment has successfully used since 1990 to sponsor cross-border terrorist attacks on India.

End of Strategic Restraint

In the past, all Pakistan-led and sponsored terror attacks across India and not just in Jammu & Kashmir had met with New Delhi's tepid response based on 'strategic restraint'. It meant that India would denounce such across-the-border acts and draw international attention to Pakistan's tryst with terror. But even the USA, despite its growing strategic leanings towards India, was unwilling to penalize Pakistan for its dastardly actions against India as clearly evidenced after the 26/11 attacks in Mumbai. Modi realised that engagement with Pakistan cannot be a one-way street and as terror attacks from across the LoC remained unabated, it became clear that it was not the civilian government in Pakistan that called the shots on India, but the generals.

The tipping point of Modi's patience came when the military base at Uri that lies along the LoC and is on the infiltration route of the jihadi terrorists was attacked on 18 September 2016 leaving 19 Indian soldiers dead along with the four terrorists who had attacked the camp. The Indian Army was seething with anger, itching to retaliate. The model for what it could do existed after the spectacular success of India's special forces in an operation in Myanmar in June 2015.

A year earlier, an ambush of an army convoy by NSCN-K guerillas in India's north-eastern state of Manipur had left 18 soldiers dead. The Modi Government—with a team of military officers led by NSA Ajit Doval—decided to launch a well-planned military operational strike on the NSCN-K guerrilla camps inside Myanmar with a 60-plus force of heavily armed Indian commandos. The Indian commando force stealthily crossed the jungle border undetected and demolished two militant camps. There were no casualties to the Indian commandos. This became the template for what could be done across the LoC.

Surgical Strikes across the LoC

Post-Uri terror attack, the 'surgical strikes' that were launched across the LoC stunned observers in India and abroad. The entire Indian force—of five commando teams—went deep into Pakistani-held territory and destroyed five camps that housed scores of terrorists, who were being readied to enter Jammu & Kashmir. Despite efforts by the Pakistani army to capture or kill the Indian commandos, they all returned safely, much to the embarrassment of the Pakistani army.

The message that went out loud and clear was that Modi was willing to respond and retaliate to Pakistan's cross-border violence. For the Pakistan army, it was a moment of reckoning. For decades, their military men had come to believe that India's best response to Pakistan's sponsored terror attacks was tough public posturing, but nothing more. The Pakistan army that controls and nurtures most groups of fanatical terrorists in Pakistan had been orchestrating their proxy war, a tool used for decades to pressurize India to 'liberate' Kashmir, in the belief that their operations would go unchallenged because India's policy makers were unable to think beyond the idea of 'strategic restraint'.

But the daring commando operation with its stunning success across the LoC not witnessed since World War II shifted the paradigm. As a face-saver, the Pakistan army threatened escalation if the evidences, with photographic and UAV-based video, of India's strikes on launch pads used by Pakistan's jehadi groups were made public. Thus, having dealt a psychological blow, New Delhi chose to give the Pakistan army a half decent exit; the dead terrorist were unceremoniously buried overnight in large holes dug by military dozers even as nuclear threats were issued by Pakistani politicians to assure its people of an Indian military aggression.

The threats meant little to India even while the USA, whose patience was running out with Pakistan, had warned Islamabad not to resort to nuclear sabre rattling. The earlier efforts by India to engage Pakistan diplomatically had led nowhere. After the 26/11 attacks, India's establishment had provided several dossiers and voice samples and other proof of the terrorists who had come from Pakistan. Each of these testaments was dismissed by Pakistan. Similarly, clear links to Pakistan were established after the terror strikes on Pathankot air base. In fact, India in its wisdom, allowed Pakistani intelligence officers an inspection tour of the Pathankot air base but they used this opportunity to rubbish India's claims.

The Balakot Air Strikes

On 14 February 2019, a bomb-laden vehicle with a suicide bomber drove into a military convoy heading for Srinagar from Jammu at Pulwama. The explosion resulted in the death of 40 CRPF para-military men, and a national outrage followed. Once Pakistan's hand in this attack was established—even as Pakistan both openly denied its role and threatened India with a serious (nuclear) response if anything adventurous was tried—Modi's national security team was examining the responses similar to the surgical strikes post-Uri terror attack. Evidences soon emerged that a large number of so-called jehadi groups had been shifted out of their bases and camps in Pakistan Occupied Kashmir (POK) much deeper inside Pakistan, fearing another commando attack across the LoC. But India's security establishment took Pakistan once again by surprise.

In the early morning hours of 26 February 2019, an Indian Air Force armada of Mirage-2000 fighters crossed the LoC with the Sukhoi-30 MKI giving them cover to target terrorist camps in Balakot in Khyber Pakhtunkhwa deep inside Pakistan. The attack came just a day after the Pakistani military had tweeted that its citizens could sleep safe as they were guarding the borders and its skies! Ironically, it was the Pakistan military that announced that Indian fighter aircraft had entered their territory and bombed the woods near Balakot! Clearly, the Pakistan establishment was shaken and lost for words. Why would Indian jets go deep inside at the risk of being knocked off by Pakistan's air defence systems, only to dump the expensive and highly accurate 'Spike' missiles on a forest? Soon satellite-based photographic evidence emerged to confirm that India's air force had achieved the unimaginable. To save its blushes, Pakistan decided to launch its fighters towards the LoC, but their bombs on Indian posts fell short of the targets, either because their pilots were inaccurate or India had used jamming devices to foil the firing of the Pakistani fighter planes.

This sham of an air attack also became an embarrassment for Pakistan, because one of the F-16 fighter jets used was hit by an Indian MiG-21, generally regarded as being obsolete. Under pressure from the US manufacturer of the F-16, since it was lobbying hard to sell F-16s to India, Pakistan made a feeble attempt to deny that its F-16s had been used. But the Indian military soon displayed parts of the Amram missiles that only the F-16s use that fell on the Indian side of the LoC! The larger evidence of the success of the air strikes on the terror camps at Balakot came from the phone-interview of the brother of the top JeM terrorist, Masood Azhar, who admitted that the Balakot camp had received many air strikes and had burnt to death scores of jehadis. Thwarting the F16 jets was achieved in all probability with accurate satellite intelligence provided to India by the Israelis. Pakistani denials along with a Chinese claim that it was their JF-17 fighter that downed the MIG-21 can be seen as a face-saving measure domestically as well as to pacify the USA, which apparently needs to give permission for the use of its military equipment against another US-friendly country.

Pakistan's Nuclear Umbrella Myth Destroyed

Most importantly, it is perhaps for the first time that a nuclear armed country has resorted to the use of air power at targets in the territory of another nuclear armed country. The air strikes have blown a hole through the Pakistani article of faith that their nuclear arsenal was a protective shield against their adventurism on Indian soil. In the past, New Delhi's reluctance to respond with military force either after the attack on the Indian Parliament in December 2001, despite a massive military mobilization thereafter, or the attack on Mumbai in November 2008 had emboldened Pakistan's military to use 'terrorism as a tool' to bleed India endlessly. Its underlying message was: 'If an Indian military response did push Pakistan into a corner, then Pakistan wouldn't hesitate to use its nuclear bombs'. However, studies and war gaming over the past decades (in think tanks abroad) have confirmed that the military brass of both India and Pakistan are most unlikely to even consider the use of their nuclear arsenal at the height of a military confrontation, as the Kargil conflict had shown. Moreover, war is a costly option and the Pakistani military echelons know that the cost would be unbearable. While the Kargil conflict had cost an estimated Rs. 5,000 crore a week, a current conflict could cost each side Rs. 7,000 crore (or $ 1 billion) a day. Thus, even a week-long military campaign would wipe out all that there is in Pakistan's foreign exchange reserves!

For India, would such a cost to finally put Pakistan's generals out of the terror business just be worth it? Perhaps, not. But a turning point would only come if the USA were to target Pakistan's generals by restricting their travel to the USA—where almost all of them have strong family links—and deny their families educational and medical facilities in the USA. This is essential if the USA means what it says and is willing to move forward in its strategic partnership with India, beyond looking at India as a market for its goods. Interestingly, it has been argued by a well-informed American author that Pakistan's armed forces wanted the return of a strong leadership (under Modi) in India, as it would allow them to drum up the fears of India's aggressive intent, and thus exercise their control over the country's polity and its depleted resources. But they never quite expected such an audacious attack.

Much of the credit for the planning and execution of the strikes must go to Modi's NSA, (National Security Adviser), Ajit Doval. A former police officer, decorated with the Kirti Chakra (India's second highest gallantry award) in his younger days, he knows both India's north east and Pakistan very well, having served there in various roles. Thus, his advice—based on a detailed analysis by India's military commanders—has proved invaluable for Modi to take the game changing decisions—like the two strikes on Pakistan-based terrorist camps—that have caused considerable embarrassment to Pakistan and, has, in turn deterred Pakistan from resorting to a major terror attack. But, Pakistan's terror-centric approach at keeping the Kashmir issue on the boil will not go away.

Kashmir and the Abrogation of Article 370

Over the past three decades, Pakistan has built up a vast network of operatives, supporters and sympathizers in the Kashmir Valley. Many of them were operating with the blessings of politicians in Kashmir who, in turn, were confident that New Delhi couldn't limit their brazen anti-India stance in the belief that Article 370 gave them in perpetuity, not only political autonomy, but the freedom to blackmail India, endlessly. There was widespread support for the removal of Article 370 from the Constitution. Thus, the Modi Government and, in particular, the Home Minister, Amit Shah, worked to put an end to this illusion amongst the Kashmiris. Though a temporary clause in the Indian Constitution, Article 370 had gained a *de facto* sense of permanence, which successive Indian governments had refused to tamper with or remove, as they believed it was the only adhesive that was keeping Kashmir in the Indian Union; but this was a fallacy. And this was the notion that was repeatedly reinforced by Kashmir's politicians whenever New Delhi tried to seek their political or financial accountability. Worse still, they used to nurture anti-India sentiments, especially through groups like the Hurriyat Conference, whose public stance and sources of funding went unchallenged.

But then in August 2019, Parliament and then the people were stunned by the sheer swiftness with which Articles 370 and 35A were abrogated. India's President, Ram Nath Kovind, on the advice of Amit Shah, gave his consent for removing the efficacy of Article 370 under the same terms that it had been enforced by India's first Prime Minister Jawaharlal Nehru. The fact that Kashmir's constituent assembly in the 1950s had never ratified and adopted it—though, having debated it endlessly—and left the Article as temporary, it could be removed or reversed at a suitable time, which was done on 5 August 2019. A further blow to the sense of self-belief of the Kashmiri elites came about as top political leaders, scores of their followers and the Hurriyat leaders were put in detention, and a total security blanket imposed on the Kashmir Valley, with a blackout of cell phones and social media. It received much criticism in India and abroad, but sensible observers were able to comprehend that Kashmir needed a change of course. The biggest blow, however, to the Kashmiri ego came when the state of Jammu and Kashmir (J&K) was divided into two Union Territories of J&K and Ladakh. The biggest opposition to this move, interestingly, came from Pakistan (that occupies a part of J&K) and China (that occupies a part of Ladakh). Not only was the abrogation of Article 370 a historical event to undo the legacy of Nehru but also to signal a new set of initiatives for Jammu, Kashmir and Ladakh.

A year after the abrogation of Article 370 and the restrictions imposed in the Kashmir Valley, despite the many pressures on the Union Government from various quarters to remove the restrictions placed on the Kashmiris, especially by its critics in the print media, a few have admitted that these very restrictions have also had a positive impact on the ongoing efforts of Indian security forces to counter militants sponsored by Pakistan, and their followers in the Valley. Admittedly, this wasn't the magic wand to put an end to Pakistan's proxy war efforts, but these restrictions have at least freed the security forces from the harassment of pro-militant mobs to enforce an effective counter-terrorism operation. A look at the official figures shows that there has been a visible fall in youngsters recruited by militant groups (based on reports to the police) and a clear rise in militants eliminated, compared to the previous year. Moreover, the existing restrictions have curtailed the flow of funds, either through banks or 'hawala' methods, to those who have in the past financed the stone-throwing protestors.

Stone throwing had been a tradition in the Valley well before insurgency had started in 1990 but gathered momentum after their Pakistani minders encouraged the people to follow the Palestinian 'íntafada' model of hitting back at the Israeli forces. The critics of the clampdown have been visibly silent on the relief to the security forces following these restrictions that have given respite largely to the CRPF who had faced the brunt of stone-throwing mobs and had a few thousand casualties from stone injuries. They've been sent in to save the Valley from being taken over by Pakistan and their lackeys. The role of many local politicians in inciting the crowds cannot be ignored either. Freedom of expression cannot certainly allow the stoning of para-military policemen. These policemen are also Indian citizens, sent out to bring peace in a land that is the mess that it is, because its politicians have benefitted in keeping things on the boil. In fact, keeping 'Kashmir' unsettled had become an 'industry' for its elites.

Restrictions on the movement of people and the lack of adequate Internet services in this day and age can be stifling. But anyone familiar with internal security duties would confirm that it is easier to ensure that there is relative calm when the security forces are not distracted by anti-national stone-throwing or howling mobs. Those who've served in the security forces in the Valley have also confirmed that good social media connectivity allows mobs to gather in a few minutes whenever the security forces were sighted, especially in a cordon-and-search operation. Those who object to that should be advised to give any better ideas that they may have in restricting the role of the militants and their minders, duly assisted by efficient Internet services. And not to forget, the anti-India propaganda unleashed all the time by the Pakistani 'deep state' through the Internet. But as promised by the Modi government, internet and phone services were gradually eased and were lifted completely in the entire J&K in February 2021. Thereon in June, the Centre invited mainstream politicians of J&K for a meeting chaired by Modi, The outreach initiative signalled a restart of political engagement since the abrogation of Articles 370 and 35A in 2019.

Those who have argued that had it not been for the abrogation of Article 370 Pakistan and China wouldn't have stepped up their hostile actions are either myopic or unaware of the strategic aims of both our hostile neighbours. Pakistan's politicians and its military would be left rudderless without their anti-Indian assertions. It helps the establishment to counter questions about their inability to address the multiple challenges of governing Pakistan; and for its military their enmity with India allows them the lion's share of Pakistan's budget. But it is China that is clearly the bigger challenge for India—with their intrusions and a military build-up on the LAC —that has clearly stumped New Delhi. It has been argued that having created the Union Territory of Ladakh and the reassertion of claims to the Chinese-held territories in Aksai Chin and the Shaksgam Valley in POK, has got Beijing's back up.

With Chinese troops firmly in place along the LAC after their territorial incursion east of Ladakh, Beijing is keen to achieve its ambitions of controlling the waters in that region. In effect, they want territorial jurisdiction over the parts of Ladakh where these rivers flow. In fact, it is the waters of the erstwhile state of Jammu and Kashmir (and now the UT of Ladakh) that could become a major reason for a future conflict. It is for this reason that an agreed formal demarcation of our boundaries with China in particular—and not just claims based on maps we publish—should become the goal for any future agreement that India embarks on, at least with China.

15

Women in the Time of Modi

Lalitha Kumaramangalam

The debate around Prime Minister Narendra Modi's spectacular second consecutive electoral victory in 2019 continues to be a bête noire for the left-liberal intellectuals. An analysis of the election results, however, shows that while the number of women voters in 2019 was only marginally less (66.68 per cent) than that of male voters (66.79 per cent), the number of women who voted for the BJP increased significantly from 2014. In fact, the party increased its vote share across groups apart from the Muslims. Even today, much to the chagrin of the anti-Modi lobby, women continue to trust the Prime Minister.

Despite the opposition's scepticism, Indian voters are not naive. Their continued support of what is termed the 'BJP Election Juggernaut' is based on the benefits they have received during the first five years. A combination of people-friendly policies and efficient implementation of government schemes ensured that, unlike in the past, socio-economic benefits actually accrued to beneficiaries they were meant for. A study of facts and figures will explain this claim better.

In 2014, after winning the Parliamentary elections, one of the first big policy moves of the NDA Government was the introduction and implementation of the *Jan Dhan Yojana* account announced by the Prime

Minister on August 15, 2014. Long a vocal supporter of using technology to empower the underprivileged, Modi put into action his ambitious plan to enable millions of poor Indians to open and maintain their own bank accounts for the first time in their lives. Using any one of several government issued ID-cards, like the Voter ID, or the Aadhaar, or the ration card, lakhs of people became the holders of self-operated bank accounts. Among the millions who could claim their own bank accounts were women whose lives changed for the better. Not only were they not required to maintain a minimum balance in their accounts, individual account holders were empowered to receive full monetary benefits of the hitherto notorious middlemen whose ubiquitous role in the transfer of benefits meant that less than 50 per cent actually reached the beneficiaries. By April 2019, over 15 crore women opened such accounts and received interest on the money deposited, accident insurance cover of Rs. 2 lakh, access to pension and the guarantee that all monetary benefits due to them would be received by them in their entirety.

Credit must be given to Modi for recognising the contribution of women in all spheres—from politics to governance, agriculture and business to sports and science, arts and crafts to banking and law. Equal opportunities for women were meticulously planned and implemented. Whether it was to appoint, for the first time, two women to the Group of Ministers (the top five ministers group headed by the Prime Minister), or appointing Nirmala Sitharaman as the first full-time Defence Minister and thereafter the first full-time Finance Minister, Modi has truly walked the talk in his untiring efforts to promote women's equity.

Another example of this was the *Pradhan Mantri Ujjwala Yojana* (PMUY), which was launched on 1 May 2016. Fifty million LPG cylinders were distributed initially to women from BPL families in order to reduce the daily drudgery of walking miles to collect firewood for cooking and simultaneously preventing numerous illnesses women were prone to from inhaling smoke from their *chulhas* while cooking. To enable the continued use of LPG, subsidies were given *via* direct transfer to women's *Jan Dhan* accounts. This scheme led to an increase in LPG consumption by 56 per cent in 2019, as compared to 2014.

Myriad other women-centric and women-friendly schemes have been introduced since 2014 resulting in the empowering of women. The Centre increased maternity leave for both government and private sector employees from 12 weeks to 26 weeks. Further, for the first time, maternity benefits are available both to adoptive and commissioning mothers—that is mothers whose babies are born *via* surrogate mothers.

In Gujarat, in 2018, the Prime Minister dedicated 1.15 lakh homes to women as a "Rakhi" gift, thus ensuring women and their children of having a roof over their heads. Similarly, in his Independence Day speech in 2018, Modi announced permanent commissions for women officers selected through the Short Services Commission in the Armed Forces. Following on the announcement, in March 2019 the Defence Ministry announced that women officers would be granted Permanent Commission in all ten branches of the army—truly a salute to the valour, dedication and resilience of Indian women. In the same year, the Centre removed the discriminatory practice of Muslim women being permitted to travel for Haj only if accompanied by a male companion, thus doing away with an unfair patriarchal religious tradition.

Keeping in mind the health and hygiene of women, the Modi Government made sanitary napkins tax exempt and vastly increased the accessibility of 'pads' to underprivileged girls and women. The recently launched *Suvidha* pads at Re. 1 will have positive effects on the reproductive health of girls and women and the resultant reduction in health costs. A healthy women work-force will undoubtedly contribute to the growing economy.

Modi's flagship, the *Swachh Bharat Abhiyan* (SBA) that is determined to make India open-defecation free and change sanitation behaviour has simultaneously freed lakhs of women across India from the onerous, insanitary, often unsafe, and undignified non-use of toilets. The Prime Minister has always believed in *Nari Shakti* or Women Power and had ensured during his chief ministerial period in Gujarat the economic and social empowerment of women. Launched on the birth anniversary of Mahatma Gandhi, the SBA was pitched to change the face of both the rural and urban landscapes of India. A hugely beneficial fallout of the SBA was the construction of separate toilets for girls in schools. The number of schools with separate toilet facilities for girls rose from 0.4 million (37 per cent) in 2014 to almost 1 million (91 per cent) in 2019. Given that in India, 20 million girls drop out of school when they start menstruating, and the lack of toilets (leave alone separate toilets) for them is cited as a major reason, the additional safe spaces of separate toilets for young girls in schools has opened up hitherto unavailable vistas of higher education and the concomitant hope of a better life for innumerable teenage girls in India.

Yet another example of Modi's resolve is the *Stand Up India* scheme launched in 2016. The Centre has ensured that every branch of all government banks mandatorily provide at least one loan to a woman entrepreneur. Additionally, the *Pradhan Mantri Mudra Yojana* (PMMY) launched in 2015, provides loans up to Rs. 10,00,000 to small entrepreneurs. Many of the major beneficiaries of this scheme have been small-scale women entrepreneurs. No collateral is required for these loans which are also available at affordable rates of interest. The 2020 Budget complements the Government's avowed intention of providing equity to women. Two of the major announcements made by the Finance Minister included Rs. 35,600 crore for nutrition support and Rs. 28,600 crore for women-specific programmes.

On International Women's Day (8 March 2020) the Centre rolled out a new initiative to help over 3 crore women entrepreneurs from the Micro, Small and Medium Enterprises (MSME) sector to sell their products on the government-run Government e-Marketplace (GEM) platform. To facilitate and encourage women from the less advantaged segments of society and to derive maximum advantage from this scheme, over 15 lakh Women's Self Help Groups (SHGs) are being trained to use the Public Finance Management System. Through this web-based online software, the Centre intends to provide easy loans to the SHGs.

And there is more. The *Cent Kalyani Scheme* set up by the Central Bank of India enables women entrepreneurs to start new projects/ initiatives, or expand existing ones. It is primarily meant to meet capital expenditure like plant and machinery, but also to bolster cash flow in women-run small and medium businesses. This scheme ensures women can get up to Rs. 1 crore at reasonable rates of interest for seven years, thus giving them ample time to maximise returns on loans taken.

Recently, the Prime Minister announced the *Jal Jeevan Mission* (JJM) which aims to provide 145 million rural households regular drinking water supply in adequate quantity and quality. With a budgetary allocation of Rs. 3,50,000 crore (approximately USD 50 billion) the JJM will see one of the biggest infrastructure outlays. Because of the massive projected employment, thousands of women too will be gainfully employed. The JJM is expected to generate huge demand for pumps, motors, in-village piped water supplies, etc., all of which will provide jobs and improve standards of living to BPL families.

The JJM should not be seen merely as an infrastructure or social benefit project. Given that women and young girls toil hard to collect and fetch water, often from far distances, the water lines to their homes will transform their lives, especially for household chores. Women will no longer have to walk long distances to collect water and will benefit from improved health outcomes, which the lack of access to clean water has exacerbated in terms of both morbidity and mortality for too long. The JJM, once implemented, will reflect in improvements in women's health, increased productivity, increased access for young girls to education, decreased expenditure on ill health, and less time spent on drudgery. Women will then gain their own personal freedom from one of the biggest burdens that has restricted their access to and compromised their right to social, economic equity.

It is a committed desire of Modi to give the 'common people' of India a decent, productive and self respecting life. There can be little doubt that millions of women have benefitted from the NDA-government policies in the last six years.

Even during the COVID-19 crisis, recognising that women will bear a disproportionate responsibility, the financial packages announced paid special attention to SHGs and women with *Jan Dhan* accounts. Using the JAM (Jan Dhan-Aadhaar-Mobile) trinity, the government transferred Rs. 500 to 20.5 crore women directly to help them manage at least a part of the socio-economic losses caused by the Government's restrictions and lockdown to cope with the epidemic. Further, 8.3 crore Ujjwala beneficiaries will get free gas cylinders for the next three months. Collateral-free loans have been doubled from Rs. 10 lakh to Rs. 20 lakh for 63 lakh women's SHGs This has/will benefit 20.3 crore households by putting money immediately into their hands to deal with the crisis..

To conclude, it must be underlined that despite the incessant criticism, Prime Minister Modi has never wavered from his commitment to give women their due. Whether it is the allocation of portfolios in his Cabinet or providing comfort and relieving women of their daily drudgery; whether it is encouraging women to become economically independent and giving them greater control over their money or even improving their access to education and other life skills, the Prime Minister has most determinedly done his best for the women of India. Few prime ministers have put women at the forefront of their governance as Modi has. As a leader of the largest democracy in the world, Modi is accredited with many flattering firsts, but his vision to change the lives of millions of women is quite extraordinary.

16

Social Media: A Tool for Influencing Attitudes

Dhruv C. Katoch

From time immemorial, information has played a vital role in preserving the security of the state. In India, a veritable treatise was written on the subject by Chanakya in his *Arthashastra*, between 200 and 300 BCE. In China, the writings of Sun Tzu, who preceded Chanakya by about two hundred years, also expounded on these principles. The importance of information in statecraft and warfare thus has historical roots.

In the present times, the centrality of communications and information technology in war-fighting capability has led to the concept of Information Warfare (IW), presenting both new opportunities and new vulnerabilities in conflict. Information Warfare had three traditional focus areas. These were (a) Denial and protection of information; (b) Exploitation and ability to attack enemy information and data systems. This also embraces Electronic Warfare (EW) and attacks on computer networks and enemy power systems; and (c) Deception by various means, including spoofing, imitation and distortion. To this has now been added the fourth element: The ability to influence attitudes. All activities carried out under IW are called information operations.

Influencing Attitudes

The great Indian scriptural text, the *Mahabharata*, gives an account of how information influenced the course of the war. On the tenth day of the battle, when Bhishma fell, Dronacharya was made the commander of the armies of King Dhritarashtra. Drona was a mighty warrior with exceptional prowess in the battlefield and the Pandavas felt that he would be insurmountable in battle. So a ruse was initiated whereby Drona was informed that Ashwatthama had been killed in battle. It was an elephant by the name of Ashwatthama which had been killed, but Ashwatthama was also the name of Drona's son. When Drona was given the news, he assumed his son had been killed and in his grief-stricken state, he became vulnerable and was killed. This was perhaps one of the earliest instances where information was used to influence attitudes and decision making.

The ability to influence attitudes is part of what is termed as psychological operations. While this has been part of warfare since ancient times, as seen by the manner in which Drona was killed, in today's environment, the overarching spread of communications has made psychological warfare a very potent tool of statecraft. The Chinese strategist, Sun Tzu, laid emphasis on this aspect of warfare in his famous treatise, *The Art of War*:

> *"To fight and conquer in all your battles is not supreme excellence; supreme excellence consists in breaking the enemy's resistance without fighting".*[1]

The above strategy, as expounded by Sun Tzu, aimed to subdue the enemy's troops without fighting, in capturing their cities without laying siege to them and in overthrowing their kingdom without lengthy operations in the field. Psychological warfare was an important component of such a war fighting philosophy.

Centre of Gravity

Along with information operations of which influencing attitudes is a subset, another term—Centre of Gravity—needs to be expounded upon. The concept enumerated by Clausewitz in his theory of war, was "A Centre of Gravity is always found in where the mass is concentrated the most densely, and which presents the most effective target for a blow".[2] This implied looking for the strongest mass of the enemy and destroying it, thus making it easier to subdue the enemy. The emphasis was on determining the critical strength of the enemy. Over the years, an understanding of what constitutes the Centre of Gravity has undergone a radical change. Today, the Centre of Gravity is viewed not so much as the source of the enemy's strength, but his critical vulnerabilities.[3] In the present age, the population of a nation is oft conceived as a critical vulnerability to be exploited and information operations are increasingly being targeted against indiscriminate population groups to influence attitudes, perceptions, and behaviour within the country and externally in favour of national goals and objectives during peace-time and in times of conflict. As an example, in the Vietnam War, the centre of gravity was correctly perceived as being US public opinion. The image of the Americans as imperial forces facilitated the fading support for the American war in Vietnam.[4] Social media plays an important role towards this end.

Role of USA, China and Others in India's Neighbourhood

Today, influencing attitudes is an important part of the war fighting doctrine of all major powers. The USA seeks to influence the peoples of foreign countries through public diplomacy (PD) efforts. Attempts to influence the home audience are termed as Public Affairs. These activities are carried out by different organisations. Public diplomacy is viewed as often having a long-term perspective that requires working through the exchange of people and ideas to build lasting relationships and understanding the USA and its culture, values, and policies. The tools used are social and cultural and also the exploitation of the media, especially the Internet.[5]

Influencing attitudes is also an important component of Chinese strategic thought. This was first enunciated in the Political Works Regulations 2003 for the People's Liberation Army (PLA) and updated in 2010. It addresses the importance of waging the "three warfares"—psychological warfare, public opinion warfare, and legal warfare,[6] committing the PRC to expand the political areas of conflict from the purely military to the more political, with the foundation for the same being laid during peace time. This enables exploitation in war to seek an early end to conflict on favourable terms and, if possible, to win without fighting.[7] The Chinese tried this in the India-China face-off at Doklam in 2017, where they resorted to threats and coercion, but as India held firm, the Chinese were forced to back down.[8]

Pakistan too employs the usage of psychological warfare to influence attitudes, especially against India, as also to promote its interests in Afghanistan. Pakistan's intelligence agency, the Inter Services Intelligence (ISI), coordinates all such activities. The United Kingdom, Russia, Israel and other powers too, deploy their agencies to promote their respective national interests. Of late, the Islamic world, though not a monolith, has also become a major player in the game of influencing attitudes, especially on communal lines. Terrorist groups like *al Qaeda*, Islamic State (IS) and others also make extensive use of social media to reach a wide audience, which has been made possible by advances in communication technologies.

The Indian Experience

Social media can influence the hearts and minds of a target audience, and cause severe disruption. Low-cost, easily accessible social media tools act as a force multiplier by increasing networking and organising capabilities. The ability to rapidly disseminate graphic images and ideas through applications such as WhatsApp, Facebook, Twitter, YouTube, blogs, and many others has put the power to shape narratives in the hands of the individual. This has both positive and negative consequences. While a more open and democratic spread of information is a necessary component to informed decision making, it can also transform into a strategic weapon in the hands of terrorists, insurgent groups, anti-social elements or governments engaged in conflict.

India finds herself in a very vulnerable position today. As a young democracy, with a heterogeneous population, the nation is susceptible to divisive forces, which seek to divide the country along caste, communal, linguistic and racial faultiness. Individual misuse of the social media is really not a matter of great concern, though that too can cause fissures in society. The real threat arises when groups, organisations and states conspire to use the social media in an organised and systematic manner to promote a specific narrative against India.

An example of a systematic campaign to vilify the government could be seen in the events of 2015, when the media was agog with news that churches were being attacked across the country. Much was made of a minor fire which broke out in a church in Dilshad Gardens on 1 December, 2014, or the pelting of stones by a couple of people in a drunken brawl in January 2015, a fire which charred a crib in a church in Rohini, and a handful of other such instances.[9] Minor theft in a church in Vasant Kunj was blown up to such an extent that the Home Minister ordered a full scale investigation, when all that had been stolen was a vessel costing no more than Rs. 250.[10] Exaggerated claims that all churches were under attack was a well designed media campaign by interested groups to embarrass the Government and vitiate the environment before the Delhi elections scheduled for 7 February 2015. In March 2015, a 71-year-old was raped in a church in Ranaghat, near the India-Bangladesh border, which falls in Nadia district of West Bengal and this too was attributed to the policies of the Central Government, though subsequent events proved that it was a case of rape and dacoity carried out by criminals from Bangladesh, all of whom were arrested.[11] It was no surprise that after a few months, the entire campaign died down, but a lot of damage had been done to India's secular credentials.

Social media was also exploited to create a rift between Hindus and Muslims. A barrage of misinformation was let loose that certain Hindu groups were deliberately targeting Muslims for killing cows. While a few incidents did take place, a case in point being that of Mohammad Akhlaq, who was beaten to death by a mob in September 2015 on suspicion of stealing a calf and slaughtering it on the occasion of Eid,[12] much of what has come out in the print, audio visual and social media, has been exaggerated, pointing to forces at work, intent on destabilising the country. Instances of cow smugglers, firing and killing villagers do not find mention,[13] but villagers protecting their flock come in for harsh treatment. In October 2018, a group of Muslim boys got into a tussle with a group of Valmikis and in the tussle, an eight-year-old Muslim boy lost his life. This was made into a case of mob lynching, despite all evidence being available that it was a brawl between kids, aged between 12 and 14 years.[14] Such incidents gain mileage during elections, in order to polarise society and cater to the vote bank of certain political parties. They lose salience when the elections are over, pointing clearly to nefarious designs by certain groups and organisations.

The social media has also been used to aggressively peddle the narrative of attacks on Dalits. While cases of abuse do exist, most cases are random brawls, where one of the victims is later found to be a Dalit. And then the narrative is blown out of proportion. The case of suicide by Rohith Vemula, a Ph.D. candidate in the University of Hyderabad in January 2016, is telling. The *Wire* headlined the unfortunate suicide as *"My Birth is My Fatal Accident: Rohith Vemula's Searing Letter is an Indictment of Social Prejudice"*.[15] The BBC picked it up, headlining the event as *"Rohith Vemula: The student who died for Dalit rights"*.[16] Many others followed suit and the social media had a field day in keeping the issue alive. But in all this, the facts somehow were conveniently forgotten. An investigation into the incident by a one-man judicial enquiry commission set up by the Ministry of Human Resource Development (HRD), now the Ministry of Education, revealed that: "Rohith Vemula was not a Schedule Caste, action by university authorities didn't trigger his suicide, there was no undue pressure from the former HRD minister Smriti Irani or BJP leader Bandaru Dattatreya in the case".[17] The party in power in the state at this time was the Telangana Rashtra Samithi (TRS), led by K.C. Rao, which was in opposition to the Centre. Yet, it was the Centre which received the flak for so called anti-Dalit policies. Obviously, there was an attempt to create a caste divide, with ulterior motives.

On an equally insidious note, we had the case of communal riots in Kokrajhar, Assam, becoming a cause for targeting people from Northeast India in Bengaluru and Hyderabad, forcing thousands of them to flee for their lives in 2012. Rumours were spread by word of mouth, text messages (SMS) and social networking sites such as FaceBook, with many students from the Northeast receiving threat messages on their mobile phones.[18] In Mumbai, hoodlums struck at the heart of the nation's pride, when they vandalized the iconic Amar Jawan Jyoti memorial near the Chhatrapati Shivaji Maharaj Terminus. If an incident in Assam can lead to retaliation in Bengaluru, Hyderabad and Mumbai, then it indicates serious flaws in our security structure which are open to exploitation by both external agencies and hostile forces within the country.

The above examples highlight how the mainstream media as well as the social media are being exploited by vested interests to create discord and ill-will within the national polity. By the time the truth comes out, certain prejudices have already been imprinted in the minds of the citizen.

Pakistan has been active in social media in spreading disinformation and in inciting Kashmiri Muslims. They have an organisation created for the purpose, which is used to create mistrust and fuel fear in the minds of the Muslim community on a whole range of issues through planned misinformation and disinformation. The project is led by the ISI. While Indian agencies are aware of what Pakistan is doing, countering the same in a world where the media is open and free is proving to be a herculean task.

The Road Ahead

In the effort to shape the information space, the 'softer' elements of power, in both public diplomacy and public affairs play the dominant role. Shaping attitudes, both for external and domestic audiences requires a strategic focus and must be carried out at the national level. There is a need for information dominance which perhaps points to the requirement of the Prime Minister also having a National Information Advisor on the lines of the National Security Advisor. Message articulation remains an important function. As Josef Joffe, editor of *Die Zeit* has written, "Today, the most interesting types of power do not come out of the barrel of a gun'" and that a much bigger payoff can be achieved by "getting others to want what you want". It must also be understood that influencing attitudes is not a substitute for capability. In advertising terms, the product has to live up to its brand image, otherwise it will lose its credibility.

Social media as a tool is value neutral and could be used by any player. Fake narratives and propaganda unleashed by hostile agencies thus need to be countered in real time. So, what can be done to stem the misuse of the social media and the involvement of external agencies in India's internal matters? Freedom of the press is a given and no action should ever be contemplated to curb it. What may appear to be a very benign attempt to curb press freedom, for the very best of motives, will eventually lead to muzzling of the press and should not be resorted to. The media, despite its many weaknesses, remains one of the strongest pillars of Indian democracy. In any case, seeing the diversity of the country and the proliferation of media channels, there are self-correcting mechanisms within the system.

To prevent subversion of the Indian public by external agencies and by vested interests within the country, the foremost weapon is communication of the truth in real time. Post the abrogation of Article 35(a) and the provisions of Article 370, a vicious propaganda campaign was unleashed by Pakistan and others, denigrating the Indian action. To counter the lies spread by such agencies, Doordarshan (DD) gave live coverage of the ground situation in Kashmir through daily programmes called "The Kashmir Truth", and its Hindi version, "Kashmir Ka Sach". Lies propagated by external agencies on the social media were busted by DD, especially when hostile actors used fake images from other parts of the world and passed them off as coming from Kashmir. More such initiatives are the need of the hour.

The spread of fake news in WhatsApp, Facebook and other portals is another cause of concern. While shutting down an app is an option, it would also deprive the millions of bonafide users from using the same. In 2019 itself, Facebook removed over 5.4 billion fake accounts, along with millions of hate speech posts.[19] Fake Twitter handles have also been removed through government intervention. WhatsApp has also limited the number of forwards to five entities and this has now been further reduced to one. The receiver now comes to know that the message is forwarded as the same is imprinted in the message. It is a matter for consideration whether the name of the original sender should be in the forward along with the date and time such a message originated. This would eliminate a large number of hoax and fake messages.

But perhaps the need of the hour is media literacy to combat the menace of hoax messages. Besides the Government, concerned citizens groups as well as popular platforms could help citizens discern between real news and hoaxes. India's legal structures also need to gear up to the challenge. If offenders are prosecuted in a quick time frame, it would help in creating an appropriate deterrent. Through education and updated cyber laws, citizens would tend to be more responsible and digital literacy across the board would increase. That perhaps, is the best way forward to combat this menace.

NOTES

1. James Clavell (ed.), *The Art of War*: Sun Tzu, New York, Dell Publishing, 1988, p. 15.
2. Carl von Clausewitz, *On War*, (ed. and trans.) Michael Howard and Peter Paret, Princeton University Press, Princeton, NJ, 1989, pp. 485-86.
3. Robert Leonhard, *The Art of Maneuver*, English Book Depot, Dehradun, 1998, pp. 20-21.
4. Anthony R. Pratkanis, "Winning Hearts and Minds: A Social Influence Analysis" in John Arquilla and Douglas A. Borer, *Information Strategy and Warfare: A Guide to Theory and Practice*, New York: Routledge, 2007.
5. Extracted from Congressional Research Service Paper titled U.S. Public Diplomacy: Background and Current Issues, of December 18, 2009, available at https://fas.org/sgp/crs/row/R40989.pdf
6. Chapter 2, Section 18 of the Regulations.
7. Cheng, Dean, *Winning Without Fighting: Chinese Public Opinion Warfare and the Need for a Robust American Response*, available at https://www.heritage.org/asia/report/winning-without-fighting-chinese-public-opinion-warfare-and-the-need-robust-american
8. https://www.livemint.com/Politics/UaBe7e7ImRmKQjBuXiML2H/Doklam-An-uneasy-truce.html
9. https://www.newslaundry.com/2015/02/03/behind-the-vasant-kunj-church-attack
10. https://www.indiatoday.in/india/story/mga-delhi-police-church-attack-st-alphonso-vasant-kunj-239088-2015-02-07
11. HT, Nov 8, 2017, available at https://www.hindustantimes.com/india-news/bangladeshi-who-raped-71-year-old-nun-gets-life-term/story-AFRJyqfFCpn1lQ7URQxcDK.html
12. https://www.dnaindia.com/india/report-mob-lynching-7-instances-which-shook-india-2639925

13. https://swarajyamag.com/politics/since-2018-at-least-20-people-have-been-killed-by-cattle-thieves
14. https://www.newslaundry.com/2018/10/27/the-mob-lynching-narrative-around-mohammad-azeems-death-is-false
15. https://thewire.in/caste/rohith-vemula-letter-a-powerful-indictment-of-social-prejudices
16. https://www.bbc.com/news/world-asia-india-35349790
17. https://www.outlookindia.com/website/story/rohith-vemula-not-a-dalit-action-by-university-did-not-trigger-suicide-says-comm/300407
18. https://www.indiatoday.in/india/south/story/jagadish-shettar-north-east-people-flee-bangalore-113376-2012-08-16. also see Times of India, 16 August 2012, available at https://timesofindia.indiatimes.com/city/bengaluru/Fearing-attacks-5000-people-from-northeast-flee-Bangalore/articleshow/15512723.cms
19. https://www.indiatoday.in/technology/news/story/facebook-removes-3-2-billion-fake-accounts-11-4-million-hate-posts-1618867-2019-11-14

17

India's Disaster Preparedness

Ranjit K. Pachnanda

India is vulnerable, in varying degrees, to a large number of disasters. Over 58.6 per cent of the landmass is prone to earthquakes. Over 12 per cent of land is prone to floods and river erosion. Close to 5,700 kilometres, out of the 7,516 kilometre-long coastline, is prone to cyclones and tsunamis. Sixty-eight per cent of cultivable area is vulnerable to droughts. Hilly areas are at risk from landslides and avalanches. Around six per cent of the population of India is impacted annually by exposures to disasters. The key natural disasters in India include floods, droughts, cyclones, earthquakes, landslides, avalanches and fires that have resulted in loss of lives and livelihood. The spectre of disaster or emergencies of chemical, biological, radiological and nuclear (CBRN) origin has increased. Industrial and chemical disasters can occur due to accidents or negligence and can result in huge loss to lives and property.

Earlier, we had no real set-up to respond to disasters. While India was celebrating Republic Day 2001, a monster earthquake shook the Kutch area of eastern Gujarat causing massive devastation. The tremor lasted for just two minutes but left nearly 20,000 people dead and around 167,000 injured with over a million structures destroyed. The ancient city of Bhuj was flattened. This earthquake changed India's response to disaster. The herculean reconstruction efforts put in by the then Chief Minister of Gujarat, Narendra Modi, helped rebuild the state. To contain the enormity of future calamities, the State made disaster risk protection its priority and set up institutions like the Gujarat State Disaster Management Authority (GSDMA), the Institute of Seismological Research (ISR) and Gujarat Institute of Disaster Management (GIDM). A round-the-clock network of over 60 seismic stations was setup to measure tremors, 50 of which were located in the Kutch region alone and now the threat of an earthquake can be determined in less than two minutes and an alert sent in less than 10 minutes. The state augmented its fire services; GSDMA developed a hazard risk vulnerability atlas, the first of its kind in the country, to assess the vulnerability of six different kinds of disasters, i.e., earthquakes, tsunamis, floods, cyclones, droughts and chemical and industrial hazards.

In a short period of time, Gujarat became one of the least risk investment destinations in the country in terms of disaster preparedness. The Gujarat model of disaster preparedness served as a paradigm for building a national response to variegated calamities. Learning from previous disasters, the Government crafted a multi-dimensional and multi-sector approach by taking measures to strengthen legal, financial and institutional mechanisms for disaster risk reduction and to build capacity for response, relief, reconstruction and recovery across sectors.

India was quick to adopt and align its priorities with a Hygo framework for action that re-emphasises the need to build the resilience of the community to disasters. The National Disaster Management Act was enacted in 2005 and the National Disaster Management Authority was formed. A National Disaster Response Force (NDRF) was formed in 2006 with 12 battalions and 23 Regional Response Centres stationed across the country. This purely, humanitarian force has, over the years, responded most promptly and professionally to disasters and in saving lives and livelihood and India is perhaps the only country to have such a dedicated force to handle calamities.

For any country to respond effectively to natural disasters, its early warning systems, information management and weather forecasting are important and these were evolved by the Indian National Centre for Ocean Information Service which provides early warnings through 300 metrological stations; it has been sending constant alerts and advisory services. The Indian Metrological Department has revolutionised the weather monitoring process with the help of remote sensing techniques. Buoys in the tropical oceans and satellite-integrated automated weather stations have been installed for accurate forecasting and timely detection and warning communication and response. The Indian Space Research Organization (ISRO) has evolved a comprehensive space base disaster management system which will have multiple applications including risk management and early warning systems for the region. Community-based disaster risk management programmes for millions of people residing in remote and high-risk areas to tackle the onslaught of calamities have been organised leading to a transformational reduction in loss of life. The same trigger has been applied at national, state and district levels for governments and civil society groups to prepare communities for disasters. Vulnerable public buildings have been retrofitted and evacuation plans are in place with a mission to reduce losses of property and lives. The National Disaster Management Authority (NDMA) has done yeoman work on all aspects and has coordinated the enforcement and implementation of the policy and plans of disaster management very effectively.

The measures undertaken over the years brought successful results which were seen when disaster-prone Odisha was hit by 'Hudhud' cyclone in 2015 and the loss of' lives came down from over 10,000 to two digit figures.

It is a matter of great pride for India that the Prime Minister took the initiative and responded promptly to the earthquake in Nepal by extending immediate help and resources. The NDRF was the first international rescue force to arrive along with the Nepalese forces. It worked tirelessly to retrieve both live victims and the dead from the debris and helped rescue 11 out of the 16 victims alive and brought out 133 dead from the debris.

Today, the NDRF has developed into a highly professional force. During disasters, it responds immediately to save lives in earthquakes, cyclones, floods, etc. In situations of impending disasters, NDRF teams are prepositioned in advance to handle any contingency. For example, for Cyclone Vardah in Tamil Nadu and Andhra Pradesh, NDRF teams were prepositioned, well in advance and, immediately after the landfall, cleared 3,000 trees and 190 km of roads in just two days in a blitzkrieg operation and restored electric poles to bring immediate normalcy in the situation. In periods when there is no disaster, the NDRF unflinchingly strives by sensitizing and preparing communities in disaster resilience and disaster risk reduction through National Capacity Building Programmes. These include Community Awareness Programmes, School Safety Programmes, mock drills, etc. So far, the NDRF has trained more than 65 lakh people in these Community Capacity Building Programmes in the country. The NDRF is also tirelessly training State-level forces like SDRFs and holding joint mock drills regularly. The NDRF works in close coordination with stakeholders. The number of capacity building exercises and mock drills has increased and the object is that the community should act as a force multiplier. The response time of the NDRF has greatly improved. And it is response which is the crucial element to saving lives.

The challenges in any emergency response are geo-climatic changes, increased frequency and magnitude of disasters, new challenges in the form of urban flooding/borewell issues/colliery collapses/forest fires, uncontrolled urban development and rapid industrialisation leading to chemical/radiological accidents and growing deforestation/environmental degradation.

India has done very well in the last five years to set the way forward by:

- Strengthening early warning systems.
- Proper vulnerability mapping.
- Preparing and sensitizing the communities as a force multiplier.
- Enforcing bye-laws in building safety.

- Inclusion of Disaster Response/Disaster Risk Deduction/ Disaster Management in school curriculums.
- Capacity building to rescue animals in disasters.
- Standard Operating Procedures for differently-abled persons.
- Planting trees.
- Follow good practices of other response forces.

In order to make the country disaster resilient, the Prime Minister unveiled a National Disaster Management Plan that is aligned to the Sendai framework. In the Asia Pacific region, India has taken the lead on several fronts. In 2015, it organised the South Asian Annual Disaster Management Exercise, SADMEX, for all the SAARC member-countries, with the focus to test inter-governmental coordination and create synergy to synchronise efforts to institutionalise regional cooperation on disaster response. It was followed by the SAARC Regional Workshop on sharing best practices.

In August 2016, India hosted the meeting of BRICS Ministers for Disaster Management where it was agreed to set up a Joint Task Force on Disaster Risk Management for regular dialogue, exchange, mutual support and collaboration among BRICS countries.

In November 2016, the Government of India hosted the Asian Ministerial Conference on Disaster Risk Reduction. The theme was "Risk Sensitive Development for Community Resilience". The object was discussing strengthening community resilience, risk resilient critical infrastructure, implementing the health aspects of the Sendai framework, promoting educational continuity and resilience of children and communities, disaster risk identification, financing solutions, etc. The Conference concluded with (i) a political declaration reaffirming the commitment of the government and stakeholders to Disaster Risk Reduction, and (ii) adoption of the Regional Plan for implementation of the Sendai Framework for Disaster Risk Reduction. At this conference, the Government of India and the United Nations Office for Disaster Risk Reduction (UNIDSR) signed a statement underlining the guiding principles towards effective implementation and monitoring of the Sendai Framework on Disaster Risk Reduction.

It was at this Conference that the Prime Minister of India unveiled the 10-point Agenda on Disaster Risk Reduction and proposed to set up a "Coalition on Disaster Resilient Infrastructure (CDRI)" among the partner countries, which goes as follows:

1. All development sectors must imbibe the principles of disaster risk management.
2. Work towards risk coverage for all, starting from poor households to SMEs to multinational corporations to nation states.
3. Encourage greater involvement and leadership of women in disaster risk management.
4. Invest in risk mapping globally. For mapping risks related to hazards like earthquakes, we have accepted standards and parameters.
5. Leverage technology to enhance the efficiency of our disaster risk management efforts.
6. Develop a network of universities to work on disaster issues.
7. Utilise the opportunities provided by social media and mobile technologies.
8. Build on local capacity and initiatives.
9. Opportunities to learn from a disaster must not be wasted. After every disaster there are papers on lessons learnt and to be learnt.
10. Bring about greater cohesion in international response to disasters.

In October 2017, India hosted the first annual Disaster Management Exercise for the Bay of Bengal Initiative for Multi-Sectoral, Technical and Economic Co-operation (BIMSTEC) countries for sharing best practices and experience involving their response teams in the form of tabletop and field exercises.

In March 2018, the Government of India organised the first Indo-Japan Workshop on Disaster Risk Reduction in Delhi which was attended by 150 domain experts from India and Japan. The workshop deliberated on various themes, viz., disaster management policy framework, risk assessment, disaster resilient infrastructure, early warning system preparedness by sub-national governments and approaches by the private sector.

The Second Indo-Japan Workshop on Disaster Risk Reduction was held back-to-back with the National Conference for promoting Disaster Risk Reduction (NCPDRR) in October 2018 in Tokyo. The theme of the workshop was "Preparing for large-scale disasters strengthening a network of collaboration in a community". The Third Indo-Japan Workshop on Disaster Risk Reduction was held in 2019 in New Delhi. The objective was to enhance collaboration between research institutes, cities and the private sector in the field of Disaster Risk Reduction.

The International Workshop on Disaster Resilience Infrastructure was held in Delhi in March 2019 and delegates and experts from 33 countries, multilateral development banks, the U.N., the private sector, academics and representatives of Central and state governments attended the event. Deliberations were held on best global practices prevailing in the resilient infrastructure, key challenges and gaps in existing practices and potential areas for collaboration.

The Joint Urban Earthquake Search and Rescue Exercise of SCO Member-States was held from in November 2019 and the tenth meeting of the Heads of Departments of Disaster Prevention of SCO Member-States in November 2019. In February 2020, India hosted the Second BIMSTEC Disaster Management Exercise in Puri.

With his untiring initiative, it is obvious that under the leadership of Narendra Modi, India, the world's second most populous country, is confident of building a sustainable and resilient country by integrating disaster risk reduction in its development planning.

Then descended upon the world the worst disaster of all—the COVID-19 pandemic, which attacked the world like a storm. The virus emanated from Wuhan in China and spread rapidly in Italy, the USA, Spain, France, Iran and the entire world. Here too, Prime Minister Modi proved to be a glowing example for the world to emulate. The deft manner in which the Prime Minister has taken on this challenge, with an unflinching resolve, is unparalleled.

Soon after the first few cases of corona virus were reported from across the world, India took timely and anticipatory action and began checking at all airports, and, in an appreciable pre-emptory move, stopped all flights from the corona virus-affected nations. Travellers suspected of being infected were kept in the ITBP facility at Chhawla at Delhi. The Prime Minister took the initiative of having the First G20 Summit on the issue virtually. He also proposed a similar meeting of the SAARC nations to draw up a strategy to counter COVID-19 and committed resources for it. At home, immediate proactive steps, in unison, were taken to enforce the lockdown including strengthening our medical infrastructure as also all other conceivable enforcement, containment, medical, safety and relief measures for the benefit of every section of society. The popular government app, Aarogya Setu, reached the 50 million users mark in the first 13 days—a salute to the Prime Minister and the unimaginable spirit of a determined India. Fool proof round-the-clock police arrangements were made to effectively execute the lockdown announced by the Prime Minister.

The measures, mentioned above, taken, were safety precautions which were highlighted in all channels and ringtones, setting up of control rooms and help lines to provide information and assistance, closure of all schools and colleges, banning of all public gatherings (social, cultural, political, educational and religious), closure of places of entertainment, declaration and implementation of Section 144, stoppage of all passenger public and private transport (air, rail and road), except for transportation of essential items, publicity and implementation of all advisories, camps to provide free medicines and awareness, supplies of essential items for the public, different stimulus packages and schemes for the lower income groups including daily wagers, free ration to various ration card holders, incentives for doctors, nurses and other health workers, setting up of relief camps and shelter homes for poor and migrant labourers, strengthening the medical infrastructure, notification of laboratories to test samples, organising factories to manufacture PPEs and stitch masks, production of ventilators, mobile health teams to screen patients and for house-to-house surveys, gearing up mobile dispensaries, setting up of isolation wards and quarantine facilities, setting up of COVID testing kiosks, experimenting with plasma therapy, using tele medicine and other measures, distribution of cash to construction workers, deferment of payment of fees of schools, social distance planning with monitoring committees for every district, block and village, setting up of containment zones and a slew of other measures for the benefit of all sections of society.

Around 200 million women from low-income groups were provided support through the direct benefit transfer scheme of Rs. 500 per month for three months in their Jan Dhan accounts. Further, under the PM-Kisan scheme, Rs. 2,000 was transferred to 84 million farmers; 80 million beneficiaries of Ujjwala LPG scheme were offered three cylinders free of cost. The Prime Minister also offered the facility of withdrawal from provident funds and close to a million workers have withdrawn nearly Rs. 36 crore . India has the biggest food security programme in the world in which 800 million people were given 5 kg of wheat/rice at Rs. 2 a bag. These have also been distributed free.

India's prompt, preventive and pre-emptive response to the foray by this invisible viral adversary has helped it cope better or else the situation would have been unimaginable.

Prime Minister Modi had simultaneously been talking to various world leaders to share experiences and implement good practices. He also held the NAM conference on the issue, virtually. India has acted as a responsible global citizen by sending medicines unconditionally to over 120 countries.

On 14 April, the Prime Minister, very humbly, thanked all countrymen for the sacrifice of each Indian as also their invaluable contribution and fortitude in the unstinted crusade against the corona virus. Having adroitly succeeded in the initial fight for life survival, now, in the effort for human survival and economic revival, a very sagaciously graded and staggered program in stage two for opening up of the key sectors was enunciated. A stimulus for industry was also announced. Assistance was also provided to small businesses and workers. The Reserve Bank of India released a hefty sum through various measures in repo rates. The Centre released a large sum for dedicated treatment of COVID-19 patients and as State Disaster Relief Fund. Full-scale operations of agricultural activities, from farms to markets were ensured. The fact that there was meticulous advance planning in detail was possible only due to the daunting leadership of the Prime Minister of India with the support of every Indian.

In the next stage, just prior to lockdown 4.0, the Prime Minister announced a Rs. 20-lakh crore economic package to turn the COVID-19 "crisis into an opportunity". Equivalent to nearly 10 per cent of our GDP, it would benefit farmers, entrepreneurs, the poor, migrants and industry, with major incentives for the MSME sector. At the same time, he also took care of the needs and welfare of the poor and migrants. In his address to the nation on 30 June 2020, he mentioned that the welfare of the poor was his Government's topmost priority. The Garib Kalyan Anna Yojana, which had been in operation for the last three months so that the poor would not go hungry during the pandemic, has been extended till November end. Nearly 80 crore poor persons will get 5 kg of free food grains each month till November. Each family will also get 1 kg of "chana" each month till November. The "one nation one ration card" system shall also be implemented to enable migrants to access the public distribution system anywhere in the country. "Under the lockdown, our national priority was to ensure that no one who was poor went hungry. The Prime Minister stated that "we will work sincerely for Atmanirbhar Bharat" and stressed on the need for self-reliance which would be based on five pillars: an economy which takes quantum jumps, modern infrastructure, a technology drive system, a vibrant demography and a strong intelligence demand and supply chain through the mantra "vocal for local". In accordance with this resolve, the Government, in record time, strengthened the medical infrastructure. Today India's medical prowess is well exhibited by the fact that our recovery rate, as on 9 December 2020, was 94.66 per cent—one of the highest in the world and the fatality rate was 1.45 per cent—one of the lowest in the world. As on 29 June 2020, India had 1600 COVID-19 dedicated laboratories, 1,055 dedicated COVID hospitals, 177,529 isolation beds, 23,168 ICU beds, 78,060 oxygen-supported beds, 2,400 dedicated health centres and 9,519 COVID care centres with 834,128 beds and had achieved a daily testing capacity of 10 lakh persons.

In the battle against corona virus, many democracies have used authoritarian and emergency measures and also called out the military on the streets to implement restrictions. It is to the great credit of the Prime Minister that he has neither invoked any emergency powers nor resorted to authoritarian measures, but proved to be a torchbearer of democracy by taking the support of "We, the people of India..." as enshrined in the Preamble to the Indian Constitution, which he quoted in his broadcast to the nation. He has reposed his entire trust in 138 crore Indians by involving each one them as equal and voluntary stakeholders in the fight against the corona virus—at the same time respecting the rule of law and human rights of the citizens. His credibility is evident from the fact that the entire country, on his appeal, resonated with clapping or lighting of lamps, not only to express but also exhibit their solidarity. And his leadership and measures were praised all across the world by the WHO, IMF and even Bill Gates. The Prime Minister's approval rating on April 21 was 83 per cent according to Morning Consult, a US-based survey and research firm. The IANS-C voter COVID-19 tracker showed that trust in his leadership jumped to 93.5 per cent on April 21 from 76.8 per cent on March 25, 2020.

In the calibrated war against this unknown enemy, there are far too many imponderables. In the absence of any cast-iron standard as to the adequate required duration of a lockdown for complete success, or the barometer of immunity or behaviour of the virus with exactitude or the correct process of recovery and, worse still, the absence of a vaccine, we are truly constrained. Managing a trade-off between lives and livelihood in the face of this prodigious uncertainty and calamity would have been no easy choice for our Prime Minister. However, extraordinary times call for extraordinary measures.

The Prime Minister has displayed, with the greatest statesmanship, his stellar democratic and humanistic credentials in this persevering endeavour with grit and conviction. It is said that true leadership is not to make someone do something, but it is to make someone do something not because you want him to do it but because he wants to do it himself. This is what our Prime Minister truly reflects and depicts —an untiring patriotic warrior "of the people, by the people and for the people."

A Viewpoint

V.K. Singh

As I look back on the seven years that I have spent in Modi 1.0 and Modi 2.0 Government, I find that Prime Minister Narendra Modi has created an indelible mark on the path of progress of the country. If what the nation witnessed in the first five years, where structural changes were made for an inclusive progress on the path of creation of "New India", the last two years have seen a historical 'New' in the pace of development. Let me illustrate this by analyzing two areas that impact National Security, viz., the defence sector and the contours of foreign policy.

The defence sector has had an endemic challenge of decision-making. This manifests itself in issues and proposals pending for a long time. This also seriously affects the procurements sought to upgrade the combat worthiness of the Armed Forces. The One Rank One Pension (OROP) is a classic example of welfare where it took 40-plus years to resolve it and it was all due to the decisiveness of the Prime Minister. In the six months of Modi 2.0, we witness decisiveness in all aspects of the defence establishment. The post of Chief of Defence Staff (CDS) has been another long pending issue. The idea goes back to Lord Mountbatten and was also advanced by General Krishna Rao in 1982. Officially, it was mooted in 1999 as part of the Kargil Review Committee report and a Group of Ministers officially proposed it in 2001. It is only in 2019 that the decision to have a CDS was announced by the Prime Minister from that ramparts of the Red Fort in his Independence Day speech.

The decision to acquire Rafale MMRCA fighter aircraft in flying and combat ready state again shows the decisiveness of the Government. A decision was pending since 2012 and except for regressive movement the deal seemed to have been stuck at the cost of combat efficiency of the Indian Air Force. The induction of Apache attack helicopters in September 2020 is a similar story. Had it not been for the decisiveness of the Government, the induction would have suffered inordinate delays. The Government headed by Narendra Modi has been at the forefront to ensure that all requirements of the Armed Forces are taken care of without wasting time.

Under the initiative of Make in India and the encouragement given by the Prime Minister himself, the DRDO also rose to the occasion and tested its state-of-the-art Quick Reaction Surface to Air Missile system. This adds to the efficacy of our Air Defence Systems and modernises the inventory of both the Air Force and the Army. As I mentioned earlier, our modernisation and combat worthiness suffered due to lack of decisiveness and these 24 months have proved that the Government will leave no stone unturned on matters of national interest and security.

The Government has also displayed great alacrity in dealing with welfare issues of the defence forces as also the Central Armed Police Force and Para Military Forces. Issues concerning rations, pay, promotions and progression were resolved in a time-bound manner. This is something that the nation had not seen prior to 2014.

The foreign policy contours show the effort made by Prime Minister Modi to create a niche for India in global affairs. The Howdy Modi programme of 50,000 expatriates in Houston, USA, that was attended by former President Donald Trump and acclaimed by several eminent global public figures, showcased the stature of the Prime Minister and the vibrancy of our expatriate community. The confidence created in our expatriates all over the world has resulted in true appreciation of India and its skilled population. The relations with the global polity have really bloomed and the outcome can be witnessed in the support we have been able to garner in various global forums. The Modi 2.0 has showcased the fine balancing that has been achieved in our foreign policy.

In summation, it can only be stated that the focused efforts and renewed vigour of the Modi 2.0 Government has opened an era of peace, progress and prosperity and in the process has defined a new and emerging India.

General V.K. Singh, PVSM, AVSM, YSM (Retd.)
Minister of State for Road Transport and Highways and
Minister of State for Civil Aviation

List of Contributors

Alok Joshi joined the Indian Police Service (IPS) in 1976 and was allotted the Haryana Cadre. In 1985 he was inducted in the Intelligence Bureau (IB) and served at various locations including Bihar and J&K. He moved laterally to R&AW in 1994, returned to the IB in 2005 and moved again to R&AW in 2007. He headed R&AW from December 2012-14 and after his superannuation was appointed as Chairman, National Technical Research Organisation (NTRO) from 2015-2018. Thereafter he was Member National Security Advisory Board (NSAB) and continues in that capacity. He has abiding interest in national security issues particularly relating to application of technologies in intelligence collection and analysis.

Amar Sinha joined the Indian Foreign Service (IFS) in 1982. He is an economics graduate from Patna University and worked with the State Bank of India for two years before joining the IFS. During his diplomatic career spanning 35-years, he has served in various capacities in Algiers, Buenos Aires, Washington DC, Jakarta and Brussels. He also served as Ambassador in Tajikistan and Afghanistan besides several tours of duty in India in different ministries. After his retirement, he was appointed to the Board of HPCL as Independent Director (2017-2020) and on the National Security Advisory Board (Jan 2019-Dec 2020). Currently, he is Distinguished Fellow in Research and Information System for Developing Countries (RIS) and on the Advisory Board of India Foundation. He is also associated with the Vivekananda Foundation and other think-tanks besides the CII's international council.

Anirban Ganguly is Director of Dr. Syama Prasad Mookerjee Research Foundation (SPMRF) New Delhi. He is Member of the Policy Research Department of BJP. Dr Ganguly was a Member of the Central Advisory Board of Education (CABE), Ministry of Human Resources Development. Dr Ganguly was also a Member of the Governing Board of Auroville Foundation (MHRD). He had his early education at Sri Aurobindo International Centre of Education, Puducherry and holds a Masters in International Relations, a Post-Graduate Diploma in Mass Communication & Journalism and a PhD in education from Jadavpur University, Kolkata. Dr Ganguly has authored/edited/co-edited the following books, *"Dattopant Thengadi: The Activist Parliamentarian"* (2020), *"Amit Shah and the March of BJP"* (2019), *"Making of New India: Transformation Under Modi Government"* (2018), *"Syama Prasad Mookerjee: His Vision of Education"* (2017), *"The Modi Doctrine: New Paradigms in India's Foreign Policy"* (2016), *"Redefining Governance: Essays on One year of Narendra Modi Government"* (2015), *"Swami Vivekananda, Buddha & Buddhism"* (2014), *"Debating Culture"* (2013), *"Education: Philosophy & Practice"* (2011).

Asoke Mukerji served in the IFS for more than 37-years, before retiring from New York as India's Ambassador and Permanent Representative to the United Nations in December 2015. During 2010-2012, he led India's bilateral multi-agency counterterrorism dialogues with the United States, United Kingdom, France, Russia, and China, as well as with countries in India's neighbourhood. He was India's chief negotiator in the establishment of the 30-country Global Counter Terrorism Forum (GCTF) launched in September 2011 in New York. The GCTF collaborates with the UN in implementing the UN Global Counter Terrorism Strategy. He has represented India in the UN bodies dealing with counter terrorism, including on the Advisory Board of the UN Counter Terrorism Center. He is currently a Distinguished Fellow of the Vivekananda International Foundation and a Member of the Board of Management of the Centre for Military History and Conflict Studies at the United Service Institution (USI) of India.

Bibek Debroy is Chairman Economic Advisory Council to the Prime Minister (EAC-PM) and President, Indian Statistical Institute (ISI). He also served as Member, NITI Aayog (2015-19). An economist, Debroy was educated in Presidency College, Kolkata; Delhi School of Economics and Trinity College, Cambridge. He has worked in Presidency College, Kolkata (1979-83), Gokhale Institute of Politics and Economics, Pune (1983-87); Indian Institute of Foreign Trade, Delhi (1987-93); as the Director of a Ministry of Finance/UNDP project on legal reforms (1993-98); Department of Economic Affairs (1994-95); National Council of Applied Economic Research (1995-96); Rajiv Gandhi Institute for Contemporary Studies (1997-2005); PHD Chamber of Commerce and Industry (2005-06); and Centre for Policy Research (2007-15). He was awarded Padma Shri, the fourth highest civilian award of India in 2015 and has authored/edited several books, papers and popular articles.

Maj. Gen. Dhruv C. Katoch, SM, VSM (Retd.) was commissioned in the Dogra Regiment in 1972. In a career span of nearly four decades, he has held instructional assignments in the Infantry School, Mhow and the Indian Military Academy, Dehradun and senior staff appointments at the brigade, division and corps levels. Besides the NDC, he is a graduate of the Defence Services Staff College, Wellington and the Higher Command Course, Mhow. He has vast experience in sub conventional conflict, having taken part in the Indian Peace Keeping Force (IPKF) operations in Sri Lanka as also operations against terrorists and insurgents in J&K and various states of North East India. He has commanded a Sector as well as a division in the North East and subsequently retired as Chief of Staff of an operational Corps. After his retirement he served as the Director of Centre for Land Warfare Studies and is presently Director of India Foundation, Editor *Salute Magazine* and Secretary General, Indian War Veterans Association.

Lalitha Kumaramangalam is a member of the Bharatiya Janata Party (BJP) and former Chairperson of the National Commission for Women. She was earlier the National Secretary of the BJP. A graduate of St. Stephen's College and an MBA from Madras University, she runs an

NGO named *Prakriti*. She contested Lok Sabha elections twice in 2004 and 2009. .

Maroof Raza is a noted media commentator on military and security issues and hosts the popular Latitude programme for *Times Now*. He is the editor-at-large of *Fauji India* Magazine. A graduate from St. Stephen's College, Maroof completed his MA from King's College, London and an MPhil from Cambridge University. He has held visiting fellowships at the Centre for Policy Research, New Delhi, the Henry Stimson Centre, Washington, DC and at the War Studies Department in King's College. He has also been a visiting professor at Middlesex University. He writes frequently for leading newspapers and did a guest role in the 2014 film 'Holiday: A Soldier is Never Off-Duty.'

Admiral R.K. Dhowan, PVSM, AVSM, YSM (Retd.) is the former Chief of the Naval Staff, Indian Navy. During his distinguished career in the Navy spanning over 42-years, he formulated many far-reaching doctrines such as Indian Maritime Security Strategy (2015) and the Indian Maritime Doctrine (updated 2015). He is the former Chairman of the National Maritime Foundation, which is India's premier maritime think-tank. Presently as the Founder and Chairperson, Society for Aerospace Maritime and Defence Studies (SAMDeS); he is both the practitioner and promoter of broader maritime thinking and fresh strategic perspectives. Admiral Dhowan has been lecturing extensively at universities, military colleges, think-tanks and academia in India, as well as at various apex-level institutions abroad; articulating his views on the changing strategic maritime perspective; harnessing the Blue Economy and the role India would play in the Indo-Pacific region.

Ranjit K. Pachnanda retired as DG, ITBP. Prior to that he has been DG NDRF, Commissioner of Police, Kolkata, ADG (Airport Sector) CISF, ADG Operations CRPF, IG BSF, DC South, Kolkata, SP CBI, Asst. Director SPG and led the Indian Delegation at the UN Chief of Police Summit at New York in 2018. He is author of the bestselling book *Terrorism and Response to Terrorist Threat* (2001). A graduate in economics honours from St. Stephen College, Delhi, he stood first in LLB from Panjab University. He is a recipient of the President's Police Medal for Distinguished Service and Indian Police Medal for Meritorious Service and six Director General Commendation Discs. He received a special commendation from the Prime Minister of India. He was awarded the IPS Association Sword of Honour at the National Police Academy and has been a national squash player. After retirement he was appointed as Security Advisor to the Chief Minister, Assam (MoS rank). He was thereafter Chairman, Haryana Public Service Commission and currently Chairman, Haryana Electricity Regulatory Commission.

Lt. Gen. S.L. Narashimhan, PVSM, AVSM*, VSM (Retd.) is an Infantry Officer commissioned in 1977. He has done graduation in Mathematics, Post-Graduation in Defence Studies and holds a PhD in India-China Relations. He served as the Defence Attaché in the Embassy of India in China for three years and is qualified in Chinese language. A keen observer of China for the past 18-years, his expertise spans international relations and internal issues, economy and defence related subjects of China. He has been actively involved in several Track 2 dialogues both in India and abroad and has authored many articles in journals and magazines. He is, presently, Member of the National Security Advisory Board and Director General, Centre for Contemporary China Studies. He is also a Distinguished Fellow with Centre for Air Power Studies.

Sarbananda Sonowal is Cabinet Minister, Ministry of Ayurveda, Yoga and Naturopathy, Unani, Siddha and Homoeopathy (AYUSH); and the Ministry of Ports, Shipping and Waterways. Elected twice to the Lok Sabha (2004 and 2014), Sonowal earlier served as Cabinet Minister of Youth Affairs and Sports from 2014-2016 before becoming the Chief Minister of Assam (2016-2021).

Satya Pal Singh is a Member of Parliament (Lok Sabha) from Baghpat, Uttar Pradesh. An IPS turned politician, he formerly served as Minister of State for Human Resource Development and Minister of State in the Ministry of Water Resources, River Development & Ganga Rejuvenation. He has also formerly been the Police Commissioner of Mumbai, Pune and Nagpur besides holding several important and high profile assignments in Maharashtra Police. Dr. Singh is a member of the Bharatiya Janata Party and also the Chancellor of Gurukul Kangri University, Haridwar. He has authored two bestselling books; one on tackling the Naxal problem, and the other a self-help book titled

TalashInsaan Ki (The Search for Man) which deals with "mankind's continuous quest in search of the truth".

Sujan R. Chinoy is the Director General of the Manohar Parrikar Institute for Defence Studies and Analyses, New Delhi. A career diplomat from 1981-2018, he was India's Ambassador to Japan and Mexico, and High Commissioner of India to Belize and the Republic of the Marshall Islands. A specialist on China, he headed the Indian expert group dealing with the boundary dispute and confidence-building measures. As an Indian Foreign Service officer, he served as the deputy chief of mission in Saudi Arabia and Consul General of India in Shanghai and Sydney, besides doing stints in Hong Kong and Beijing. He was India's representative to the First Committee at the UN from 1992-95, dealing with disarmament and international security. On deputation to India's National Security Council Secretariat for four years, he anchored national security policy and strategic dialogues with counterpart organisations around the world. He has rich experience in dealing with security challenges in India's extended neighbourhood, terrorism and extremism, maritime security, defence reforms and modernisation, infrastructure and connectivity. Amb. Chinoy contributes extensively to newspapers and journals, besides lecturing in India and overseas.

T.C.A. Raghavan is a former Indian diplomat. He served as the Indian High Commissioner to Pakistan from 2013 to 2015 and as the Deputy High Commissioner in Islamabad from 2003 to 2007. His previous diplomatic assignments include postings in Bhutan, Kuwait, Singapore and the UK. Dr. Raghavan has a PhD in History from Jawaharlal Nehru University, New Delhi. He is the author of the books *Attendant Lords: Bairam Khan and Abdur Rahim, Courtiers and Poets in Mughal India* (2017) and *The People Next Door: The Curious History of India's Relations with Pakistan* (2017).

Uttam Kumar Sinha is a leading commentator on trans-boundary water issues, climate change, and the Arctic region. He currently works at the Manohar Parrikar Institute for Defence Studies and Analyses and is the managing editor of *Strategic Analysis* published by Routledge. He is a recipient of many fellowships and leadership programmes including senior fellow at the Nehru Memorial Museum and Library (2018-2020); academic visitor at the Harvard Kennedy School (2015); Chevening 'Gurukul' leadership at the London School of Economics and Political Science (2008). His books include *Indus Basin Interrupted: A History of Territory and Politics from Alexander to Nehru* (Penguin, 2021); *Riverine Neighbourhood: Hydro-politics in South Asia* (2016) and *Climate Change Narrative: Reading the Arctic* (2014). His edited and co-edited volumes include *The Modi Doctrine: New Paradigms in India's Foreign Policy* (2016); *Non-Traditional Security Challenges in Asia: Approaches and Responses* (Routledge, 2015); *Arctic: Commerce, Governance and Policy* (Routledge, 2015) and *Emerging Strategic Trends in Asia* (2015).

Index

*